FastTrack
MUSIC INSTRUCTION

Keyboard Chords & Scales

To access audio visit:
www.halleonard.com/mylibrary
Enter Code
4193-6492-3521-9436

ISBN 978-0-7935-7418-6

HAL•LEONARD®
CORPORATION
7777 W. BLUEMOUND RD. P.O. BOX 13819 MILWAUKEE, WI 53213

Visit Hal Leonard online at
www.halleonard.com

INTRODUCTION

Why you bought this book...

Hello again. We say "again" because we're assuming that you've already been through **FastTrack™ Keyboard 1** and **2**. (At the very least, **Book 1**.) If so—terrific! You've decided to keep learning your instrument and you're ready for this supplemental book.

This book provides five important things:

 Basic chord theory

 Easy-find index of over 700 different chord diagrams

 Basic scale and mode theory

 Patterns for 5 scales and 7 modes

 Special "Jam Session" using the chords and scales introduced

> IMPORTANT: This book is a reference book (much like a dictionary) and should not take the place of a keyboard instruction book. That being said, please go through **FastTrack Keyboard 1** and **2** (or at least act like it, so we'll stop nagging).

Remember, if your hands hurt, take a break. Some of these chords require some stretching, and the scales need nimble fingers. With practice and patience, you can learn them all (and avoid cramping).

So, when you're ready, power "on," crack your knuckles, and let's learn some chords and scales...

ABOUT THE AUDIO

Glad you noticed the added bonus—Audio! Each of the tracks in the special "Jam Session" is included, so you can hear how it sounds and play along. Take a listen whenever you see this symbol: 🔊

Each audio example is preceded by one measure of "clicks" to indicate the tempo and meter. Pan right to hear the keyboard emphasized. Pan left to hear the accompaniment emphasized. As you become more confident, try playing along with the rest of the band.

WHERE TO FIND THINGS

PRIMER — 4

What's a chord? — 4
Table of chord suffixes — 4
Building chords: Intervals — 5
Everything's relative — 5
Table of intervals — 6
Basic chord types — 7
Building to scale — 8
What's an inversion? — 9
Using the chord diagrams — 10

CHORDS — 11

no suffix	major	12
m, min, −	minor	14
+, aug, (♯5)	augmented	16
dim, °	diminished	18
sus, sus4	suspended fourth	20
(♭5)	flatted fifth	22
6	sixth	24
m6,	minor sixth	26
7	seventh	28
m7, min7, -7	minor seventh	30
maj7, M7	major seventh	32
7♯5, +7	seventh, sharp fifth	34
dim7, °7	diminished seventh	36
7♭5	seventh, flat fifth	38
m7♭5	minor seventh, flat fifth	40
6/9	sixth, added ninth	42
7♯9	seventh, sharp ninth	43
7♭9	seventh, flat ninth	44
9	ninth	45
m9, min9	minor ninth	46
11	eleventh	47
m11	minor eleventh	48
13	thirteenth	49

SCALES — 50

Building scales — 51
Explanation of patterns — 51
Fingering — 52
Major scale — 53
Minor scale — 54
Harmonic minor scale — 55
Melodic minor scale — 56
Blues scale — 57

MODES — 58

Patterns — 59

JAM SESSION — 60

Heavenly Ballad — 61
Medium Rock — 61
Wall of Fame — 61
Wild and Crazy — 61
Full Deck Shuffle — 62
Generic Pop — 62
Funky Feeling — 62
Don't Stop — 62
Smooth Jazz — 62
Overtime — 62
Nashville Dreamin' — 63
Heavy Rock — 63
Alley Cat — 63
Fusion — 63
South of the Border — 63
Scare Us — 64
Swing It! — 64
Metal Mix — 64
Rock 'n' Roll — 64
Outta Here — 64

LET'S DIVE RIGHT IN

What's a chord?

A **chord** is defined as three or more notes played at the same time. Chords provide the **harmony** that supports the melody of a song.

Sometimes chords are indicated by **chord symbols**, written (usually) above the musical staff. A chord symbol is simply an abbreviation for the name of that chord. For example, the symbol for an **F-sharp minor seven** chord would be **F♯m7**.

Let's get organized...

A chord symbol tells us two things about the chord—**root** and **type**:

1. The **root** gives the chord its name. For example, the root of a C major chord is the note C, the root of an F♯m7 chord is F♯ (Simple Simon!):

2. The chord's **type** is indicated by a **suffix** (m, 7, sus, maj9). There are lots of chord types and suffixes, but there's no need to panic—with a little practice, they're easy to recognize. This book groups all the chords by their type, so keep this list handy:

Suffix	Chord Type	Suffix	Chord Type
no suffix	major	m7, min7, -7	minor seventh
m, min, -	minor	7♯5, +7	seventh, sharp fifth
+, aug, (♯5)	augmented	7♭5, 7(-5)	seventh, flat fifth
dim, °	diminished	m7♭5, m7(-5)	minor seventh, flat fifth
sus, sus4	suspended fourth	7♭9, 7(-9)	seventh, flat ninth
♭5, -5	flatted fifth	7♯9	seventh, sharp ninth
6	sixth	9	ninth
m6, -6	minor sixth	m9	minor ninth
6/9	sixth, added ninth	11	eleventh
7, dom7	seventh	m11	minor eleventh
dim7, °7	diminished seventh	13	thirteenth
maj7, M7	major seventh		

Of course, you may run across other types of chords from time to time (or you may create your own), but the ones listed above are the most common.

BUILDING CHORDS
(...and you don't need a hammer!)

Chords are built from simple "building blocks" called **intervals**. An interval is the distance between any two notes. Here's a look at the basic intervals, using C as a root:

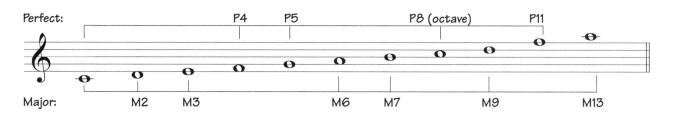

Notice that these intervals are divided into two groups—**major (M)** and **perfect (P)**. EASY TO REMEMBER: 4ths, 5ths, octaves and 11ths are perfect; all other intervals are major.

Everything's relative...

An interval can be altered by raising or lowering the number of **steps** between the two notes. How a major or perfect interval is changed determines the resulting interval category: **major, minor, perfect, augmented** and **diminished**. These categories are related in the following ways:

A **major** interval lowered one half step is a **minor** interval.
A **minor** interval becomes **diminished** when made smaller.

A **major** or **perfect** interval raised one half step is an **augmented** interval.

A **perfect** interval lowered one half step is a **diminished** interval.

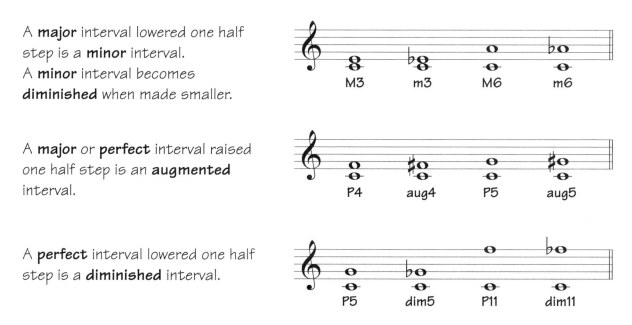

An interval's **type** is determined by the number of steps between the two notes. Review the following chart and get to know all of the interval types...

HELPFUL REMINDER: On your keyboard (or anyone else's), from one key to the next closest key (whether black or white) equals one **half step**; two keys apart equals one **whole step**.

Interval	Abbreviation	Steps	Pitches	Interval	Abbreviation	Steps	Pitches
unison	unis	none		major sixth	M6	4 1/2	
minor second	m2	half		augmented sixth*	aug6	5	
major second	M2	whole		minor seventh*	m7	5	
augmented second*	aug2	1 1/2		major seventh	M7	5 1/2	
minor third *	m3	1 1/2		perfect octave	P8	6	
major third	M3	2		minor ninth	m9	6 1/2	
perfect fourth	P4	2 1/2		major ninth	M9	7	
augmented fourth*	aug4	3		augmented ninth	aug9	7 1/2	
diminished fifth*	dim5	3		perfect eleventh	P11	8 1/2	
perfect fifth	P5	3 1/2		augmented eleventh	aug11	9	
augmented fifth*	aug5	4		minor thirteenth	m13	10 1/2	
minor sixth*	m6	4		major thirteenth	M13	11	

* NOTE: As with sharps and flats, some intervals may sound the same but be written two ways (for example, aug4 and dim5). Notes or intervals that sound the same but are written differently are called **enharmonic equivalents**.

One step further...

Once you understand (and hopefully memorize) interval types, building chords is easy—simply add intervals to the chord's root note. The type of intervals used determines the resulting **chord type**. Let's start by learning some basic three-note chord types, again built on a C root:

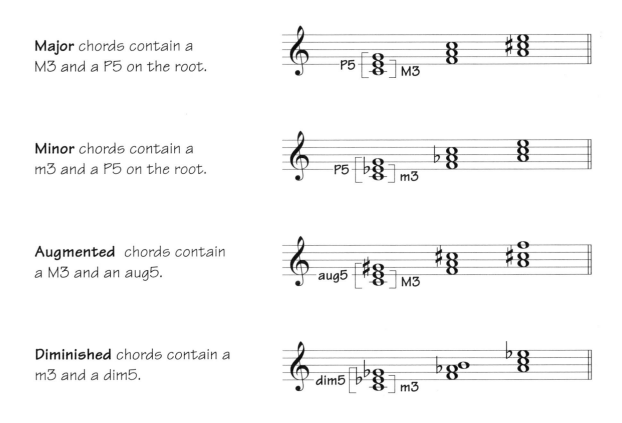

Major chords contain a M3 and a P5 on the root.

Minor chords contain a m3 and a P5 on the root.

Augmented chords contain a M3 and an aug5.

Diminished chords contain a m3 and a dim5.

Get familiar with these basic chord types, and then build tons of other chords simply by adding, subtracting, augmenting, or diminishing intervals.

Feeling double-sharp?

An important thing to know as you learn to build chords is the idea of the double sharp (✕) and double flat (♭♭). These will occur every now and then when a note that is already sharp (or flat) is altered by a half-step. For example, the fifth of a B major chord is F♯. An augmented B chord would raise the F♯ a half step to F✕ (which is actually the note G).

BUILDING TO SCALE

The notes of a chord can also be determined by assigning a numeric **formula**, indicating the tones used from the major scale. For example, based on the C major scale, 1-♭3-5 would mean play the root (C), a flatted third (E♭), and the fifth (G)—a C minor chord!

The chart below is a construction summary of the many different chord types (based on the key of C only):

C MAJOR SCALE = C-D-E-F-G-A-B-C

Symbol	Type	Formula	Note names
C	major	1-3-5	C-E-G
Cm	minor	1-♭3-5	C-E♭-G
C+	augmented	1-3-♯5	C-E-G♯
Cdim	diminished	1-♭3-♭5	C-E♭-G♭
Csus2	suspended second	1-2-5	C-D-G
Csus4	suspended fourth	1-4-5	C-F-G
C(add9)	added ninth	1-3-5-9	C-E-G-D
Cm(add9)	minor added ninth	1-♭3-5-9	C-E♭-G-D
C6	sixth	1-3-5-6	C-E-G-A
Cm6	minor sixth	1-♭3-5-6	C-E♭-G-A
C6/9	sixth, added ninth	1-3-5-6-9	C-E-G-A-D
Cm6/9	minor sixth, added ninth	1-♭3-5-6-9	C-E♭-G-A-D
C7	seventh	1-3-5-♭7	C-E-G-B♭
Cdim7	diminished seventh	1-♭3-♭5-♭♭7	C-E♭-G♭-B♭♭
C7sus4	seventh, suspended fourth	1-4-5-♭7	C-F-G-B♭
Cmaj7	major seventh	1-3-5-7	C-E-G-B
Cm7	minor seventh	1-♭3-5-♭7	C-E♭-G-B♭
Cm(maj7)	minor, major seventh	1-♭3-5-7	C-E♭-G-B
Cmaj7♭5	major seventh, flat fifth	1-3-♭5-7	C-E-G♭-B
Cm7♭5	minor seventh, flat fifth	1-♭3-♭5-♭7	C-E♭-G♭-B♭
C7♯5	seventh, sharp fifth	1-3-♯5-♭7	C-E-G♯-B♭
C7♭5	seventh, flat fifth	1-3-♭5-♭7	C-E-G♭-B♭
C7♭9	seventh, flat ninth	1-3-5-♭7-♭9	C-E-G-B♭-D♭
C7♯9	seventh, sharp ninth	1-3-5-♭7-♯9	C-E-G-B♭-D♯
C7♯5(♭9)	seventh, sharp fifth, flat ninth	1-3-♯5-♭7-♭9	C-E-G-B♭-D♯
C9	ninth	1-3-5-♭7-9	C-E-G-B♭-D
Cmaj9	major ninth	1-3-5-7-9	C-E-G-B-D
Cm9	minor ninth	1-♭3-5-♭7-9	C-E♭-G-B♭-D
C11	eleventh	1-5-♭7-9-11	C-E-G-B♭-D-F
Cm11	minor eleventh	1-♭3-5-♭7-9-11	C-E♭-G-B♭-D-F
C13	thirteenth	1-3-5-♭7-9-13	C-E-G-B♭-D-F-A

Alright already!

☞ Don't get too bogged down with all this "theory" stuff. Just look up the chords you need and learn to play them. Heck, make up your own chords—if it sounds good, play it! If you come across a chord type not listed in this book (and you will eventually), either build the chord with the intervals named in the suffix, or reduce it to a more common seventh or ninth chord.

WHAT'S AN INVERSION?

Unlike roots on trees, a chord's root isn't always the bottom note. The notes of a chord can be rearranged but still produce the same chord type. This rearrangement (or repositioning) of notes is called an inversion.

The number of inversions possible depends on the number of notes in the chord. For example, a three-note chord has a root position and two inversions, a four-note chord has three inversions, and so on...

Root Position

Just like it sounds—put the root as the bottom note of the chord:

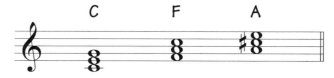

1st Inversion

Simply take the root and put it on top (one octave higher).

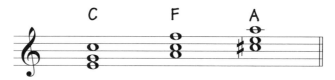

2nd Inversion

Take the next lowest note and put it one octave higher (above the root):

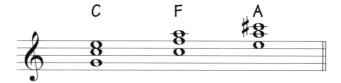

Decisions, decisions...

Although in theory you may use any of the inversions in any situation, you should choose an inversion based on two things:

1 **Hand position.** Try to use an inversion that keeps your hand in a close proximity to the notes of the chords played before and after. This will make chord progressions and changes sound smoother.

2 **Leading tone.** Generally speaking, the top-note of the chord will be heard above the rest. If you play C in 1st inversion, you'll hear the C note most dominantly. Generally, the melody note is on top of the chord.

One more thing...

Here's how to read the chord diagrams for all the three- and four-note chords (pages 12 through 41):

Notes on white keys are shaded.

Notes on black keys are circled.

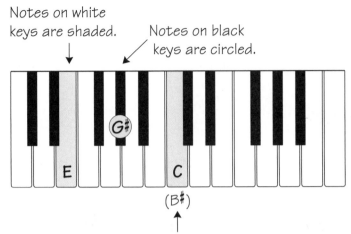

Notes in parentheses are the theoretical spelling for that chord (such as double sharps, etc.), but we've put the simpler note names on the actual diagram.

REMINDER: Chords can be played with either the left hand or right hand or both. Try them all sorts of ways in all possible inversions.

So many notes, so few fingers...

Many chords contain more notes than can easily be played with one hand. For these bigger chords (pages 42 through 48), the diagram shows all the notes of the chord. But don't hurt yourself—try a two-hand approach. For example:

All the notes in a C13 chord

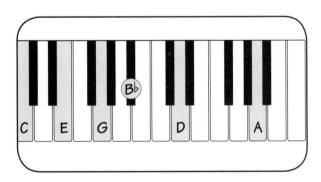

Play it like this...

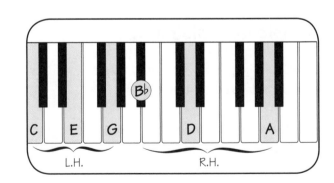

Have fun!

CHORDS

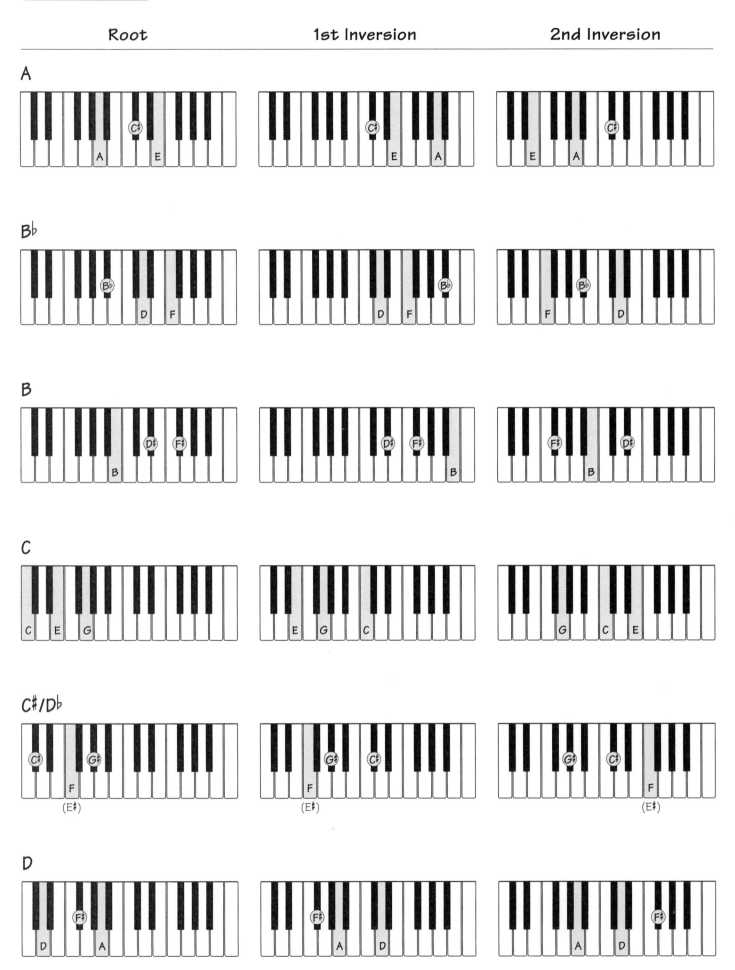

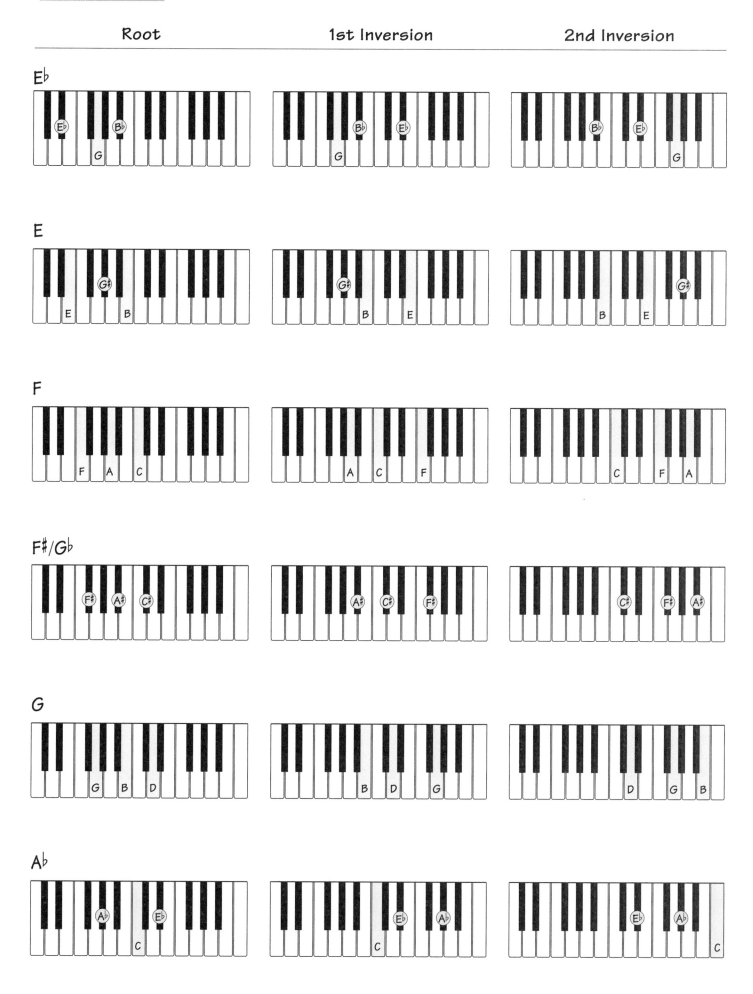

Minor

	Root	1st Inversion	2nd Inversion

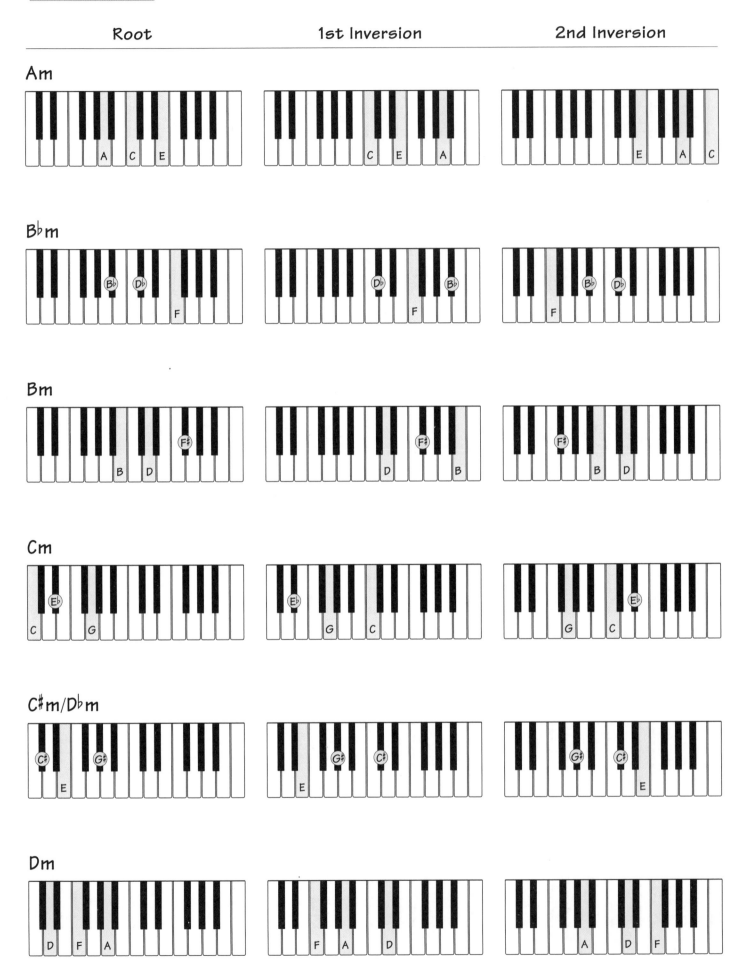

Am

B♭m

Bm

Cm

C♯m/D♭m

Dm

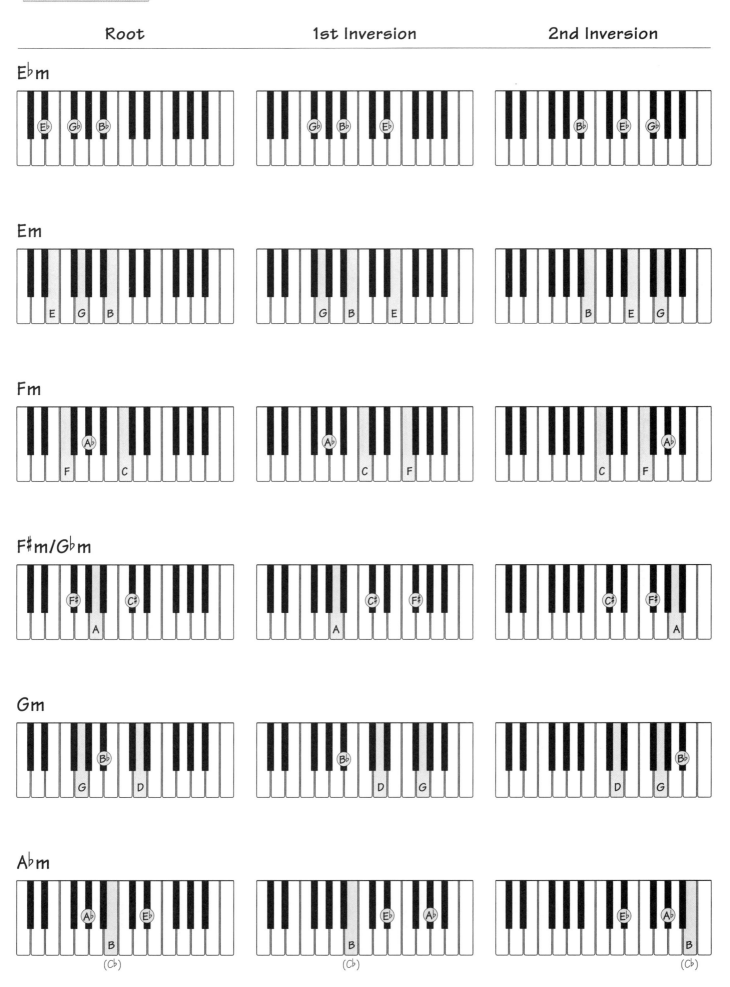

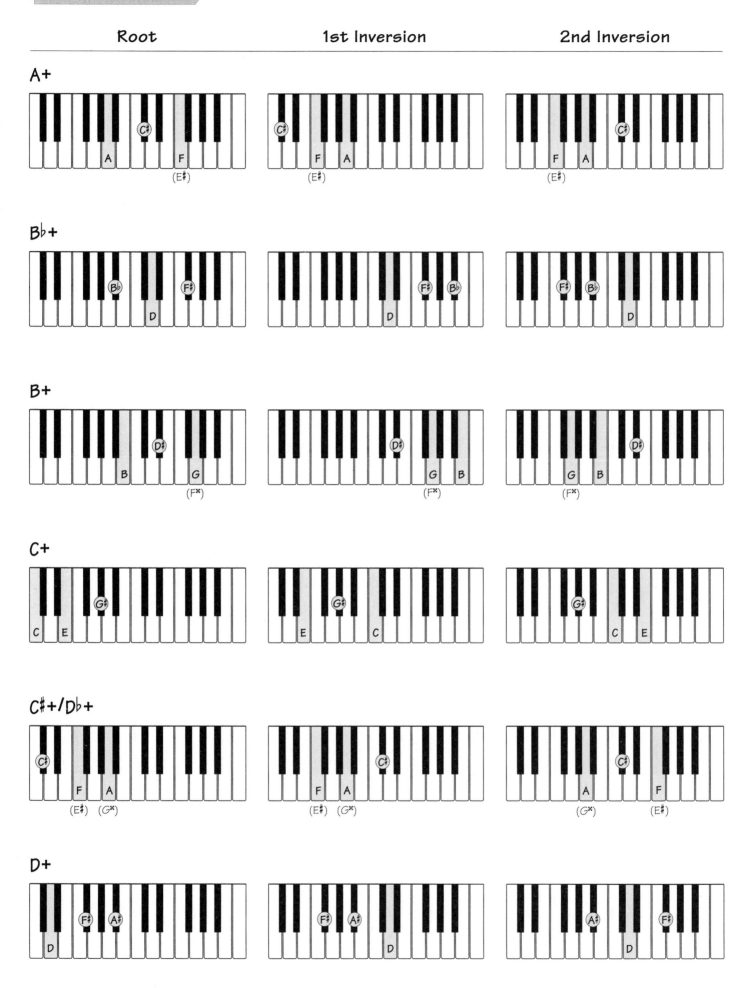

Root	1st Inversion	2nd Inversion

Eb+

E+

F+

F#+/Gb+

G+

Ab+

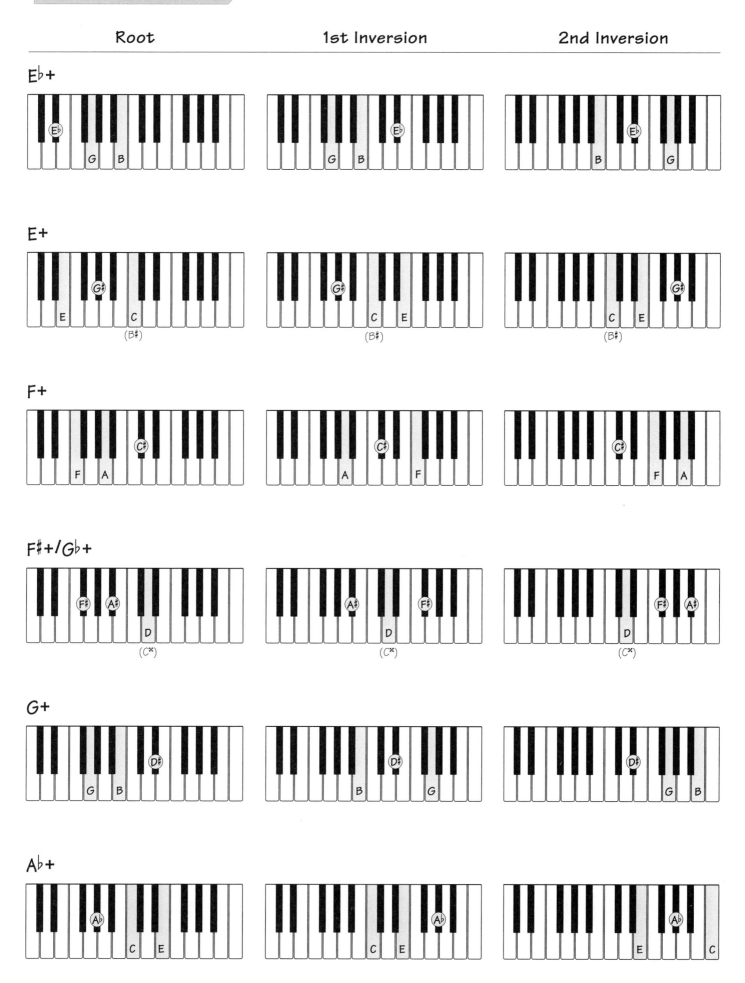

Diminished

	Root	1st Inversion	2nd Inversion

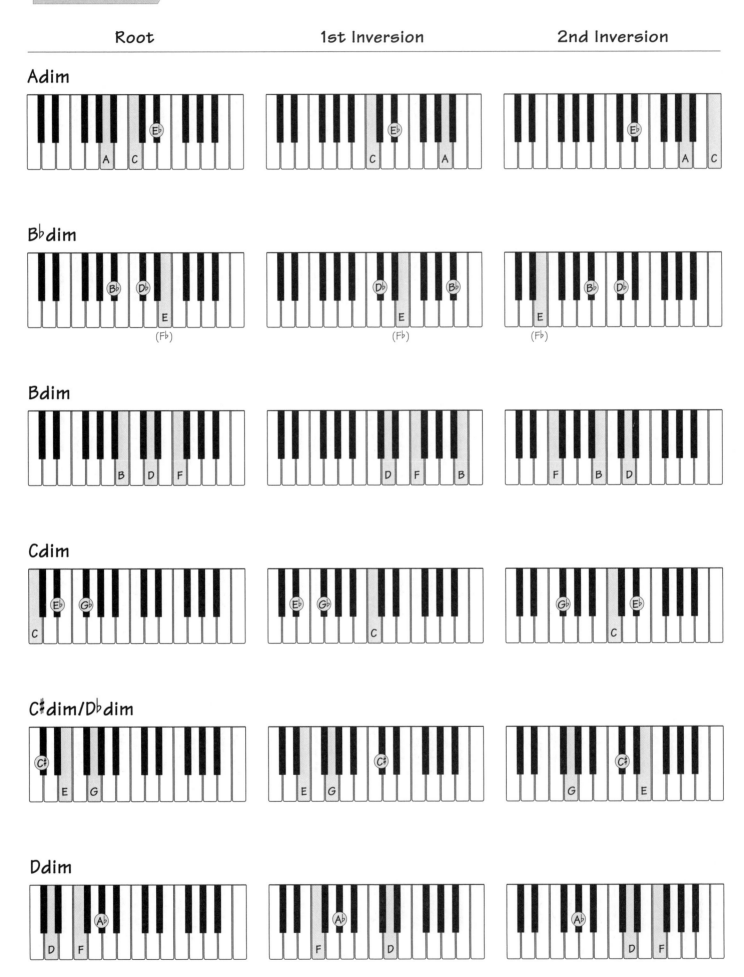

Adim

B♭dim

Bdim

Cdim

C♯dim/D♭dim

Ddim

Root	1st Inversion	2nd Inversion

E♭dim

Edim

Fdim

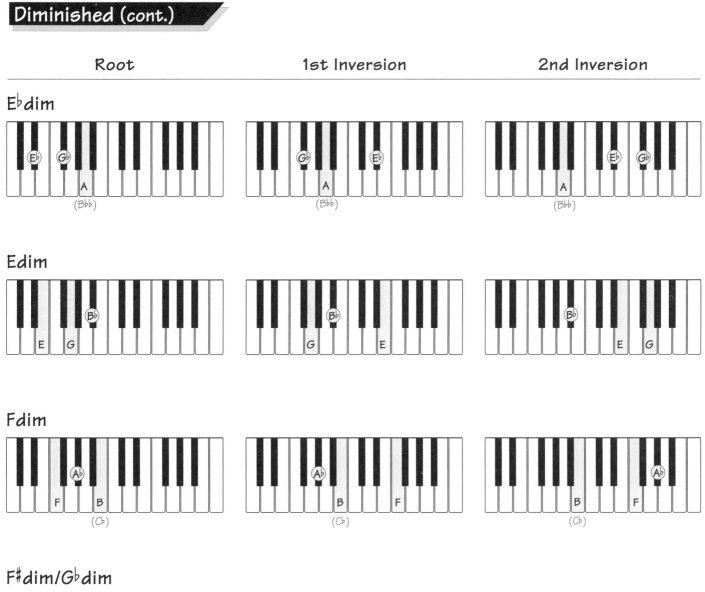

F#dim/G♭dim

Gdim

A♭dim

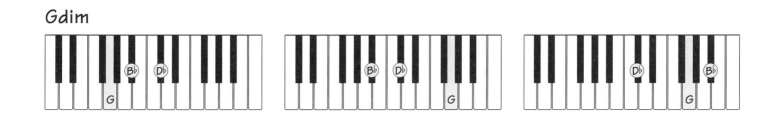

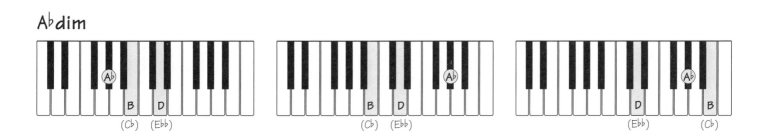

Suspended Fourth

Root	1st Inversion	2nd Inversion

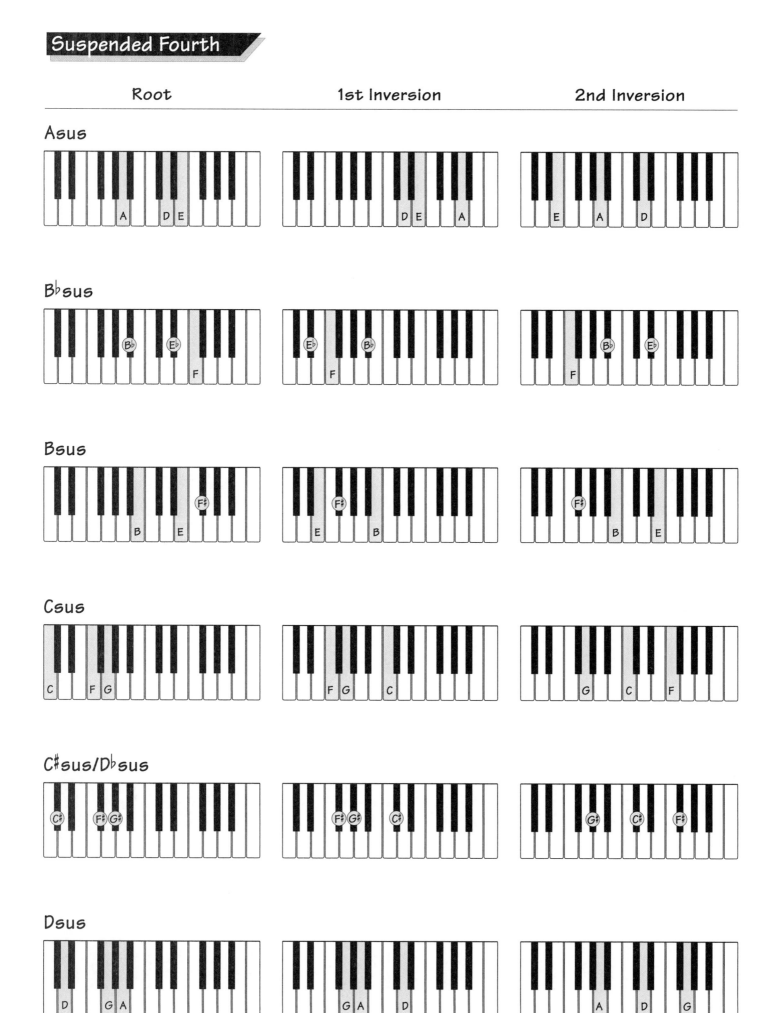

Asus

B♭sus

Bsus

Csus

C#sus/D♭sus

Dsus

Suspended Fourth (cont.)

Root	1st Inversion	2nd Inversion

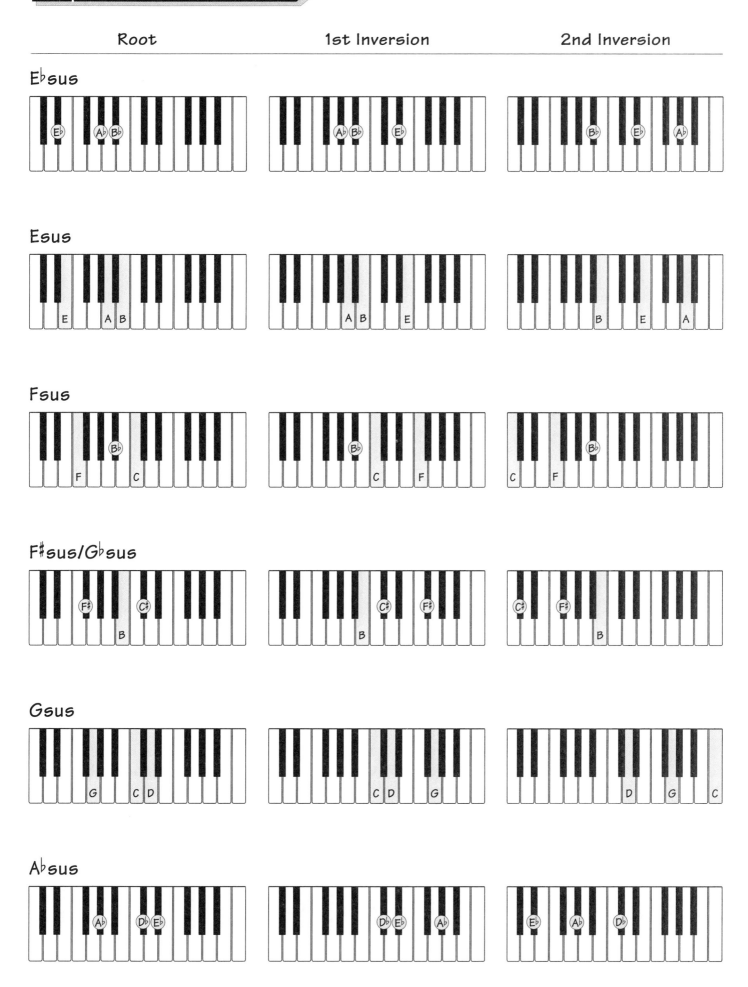

E♭sus

Esus

Fsus

F♯sus/G♭sus

Gsus

A♭sus

Flatted Fifth

Root	1st Inversion	2nd Inversion

A(♭5)

B♭(♭5)

B(♭5)

C(♭5)

C♯(♭5)/D♭(♭5)

D(♭5)

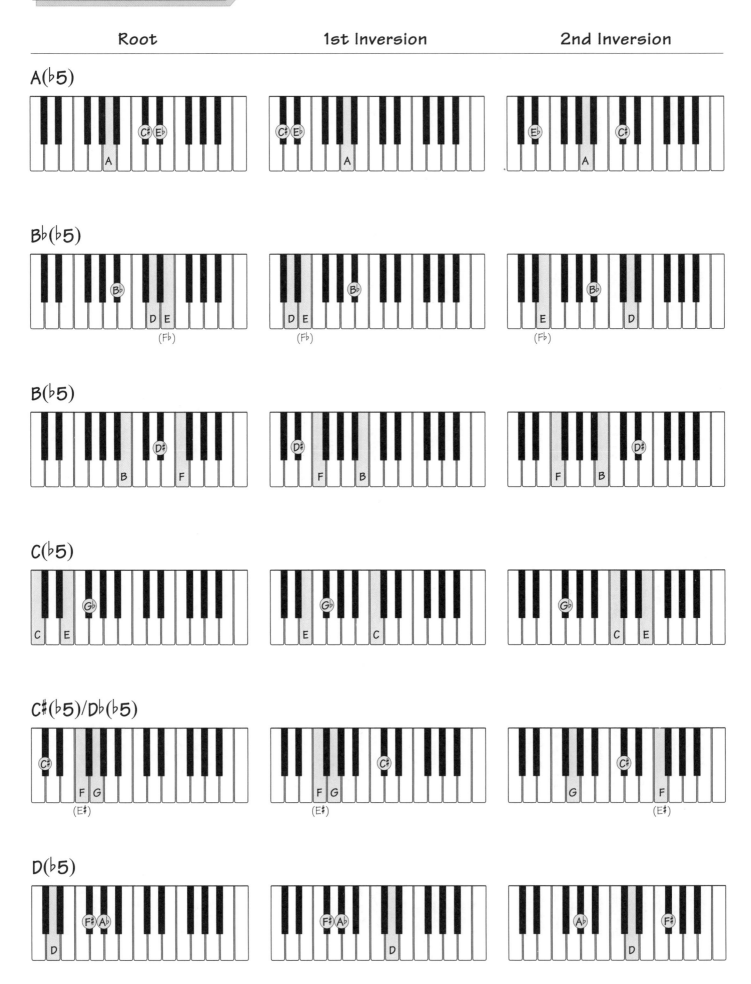

| | Root | 1st Inversion | 2nd Inversion |

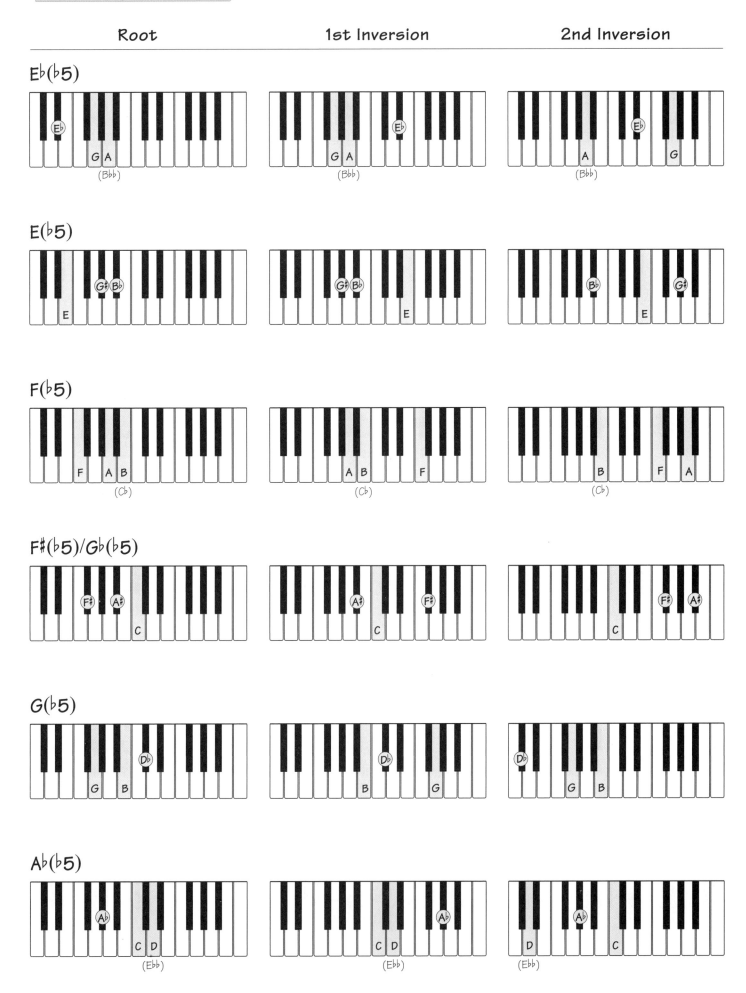

Root	1st Inversion	2nd Inversion	3rd Inversion

A6

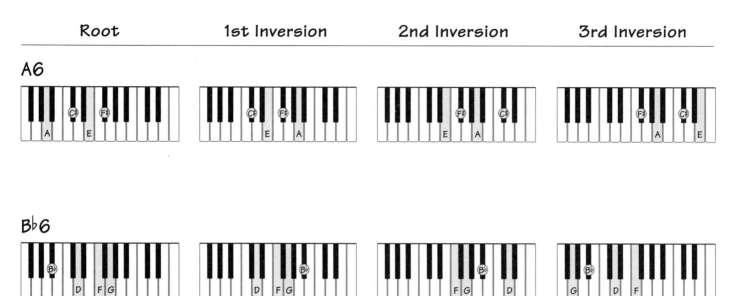

B♭6

B6

C6

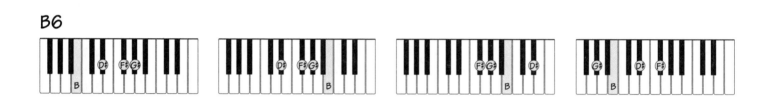

C♯6/D♭6

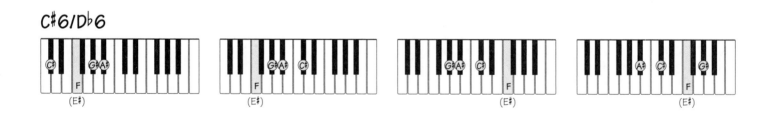

D6

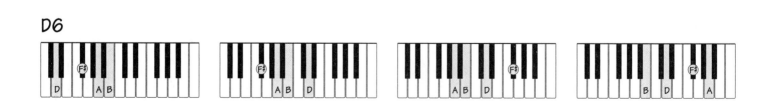

Root	1st Inversion	2nd Inversion	3rd Inversion

E♭6

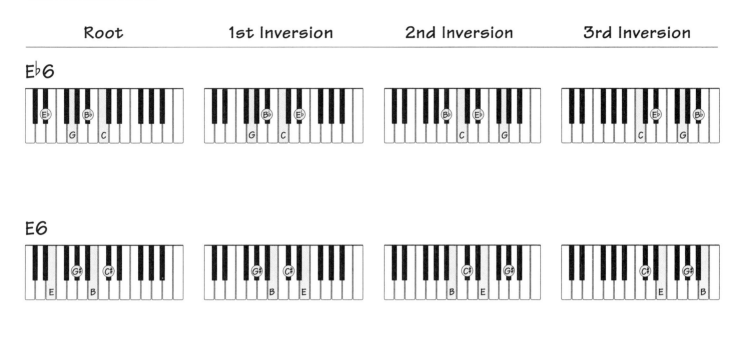

E6

F6

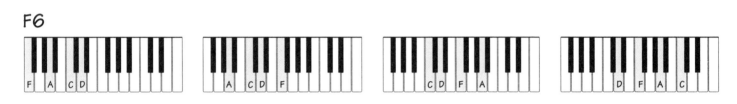

F♯6/G♭6

G6

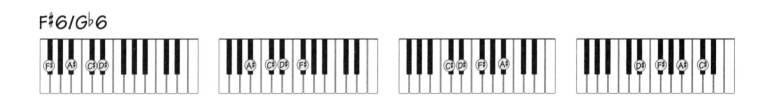

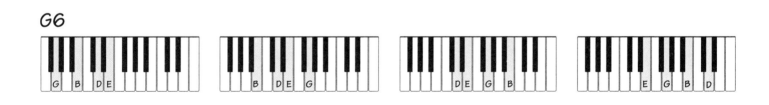

A♭6

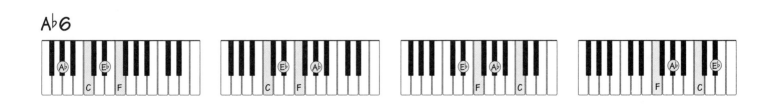

	Root	1st Inversion	2nd Inversion	3rd Inversion

Am6

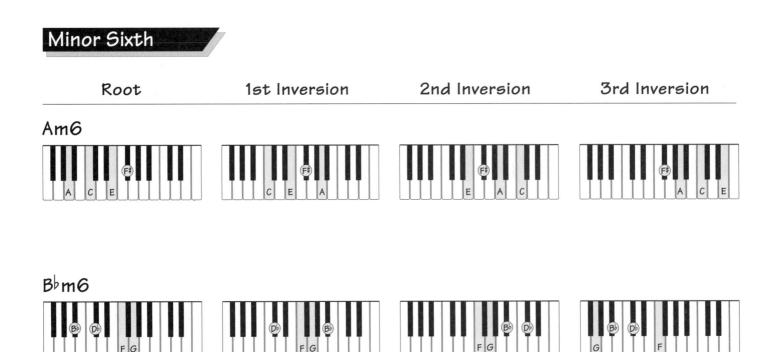

B♭m6

Bm6

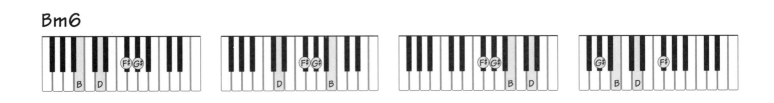

Cm6

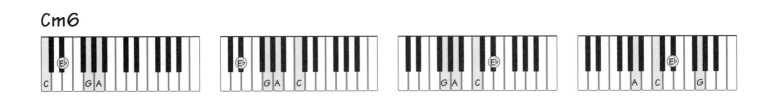

C#m6/D♭m6

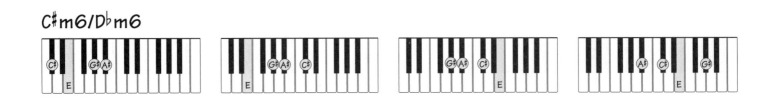

Dm6

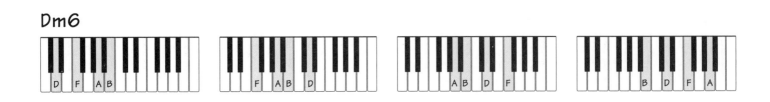

| Root | 1st Inversion | 2nd Inversion | 3rd Inversion |

E♭m6
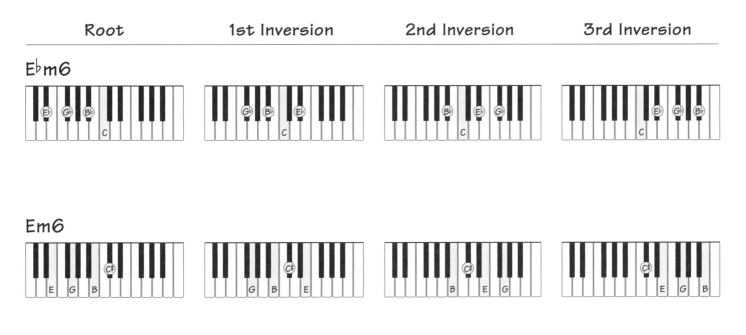

Em6

Fm6

F♯m6/G♭m6

Gm6

A♭m6
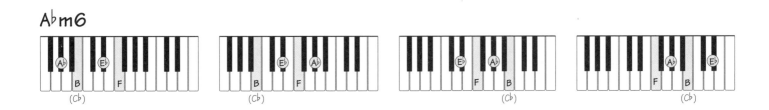

Root	1st Inversion	2nd Inversion	3rd Inversion

A7
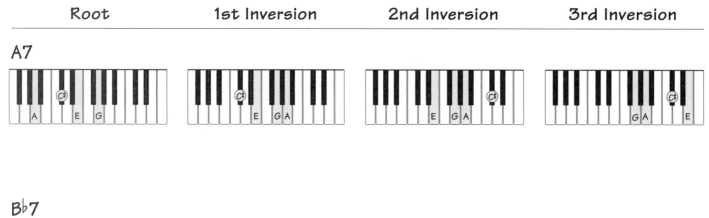

B♭7
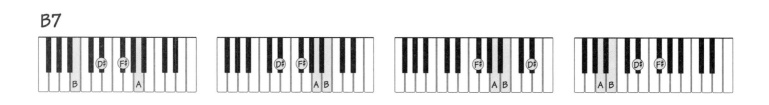

B7
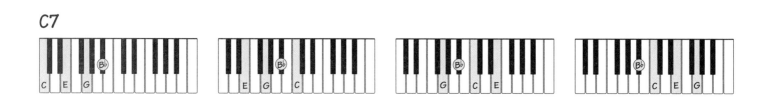

C7
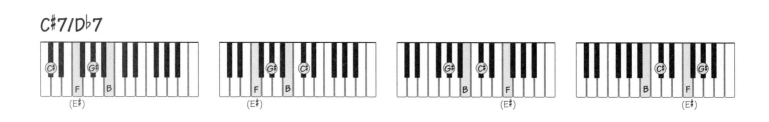

C#7/D♭7
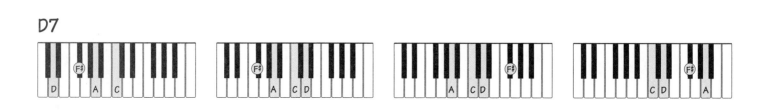

D7
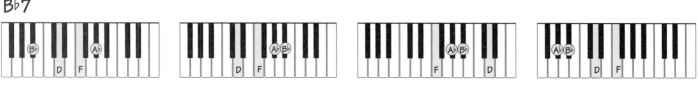

Root	1st Inversion	2nd Inversion	3rd Inversion

E♭7

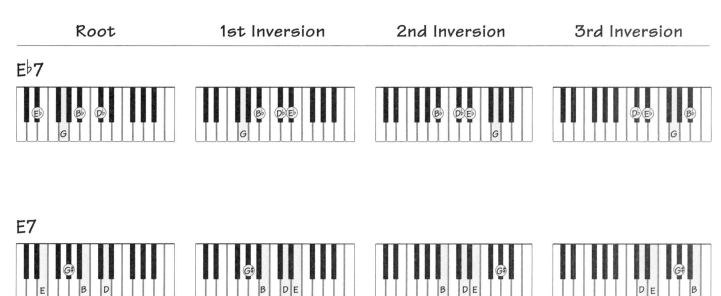

E7

F7

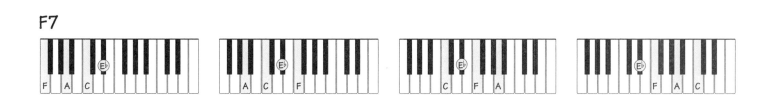

F♯7/G♭7

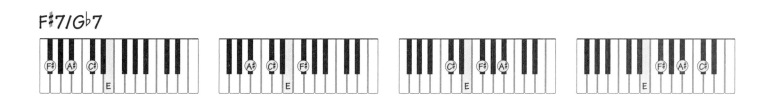

G7

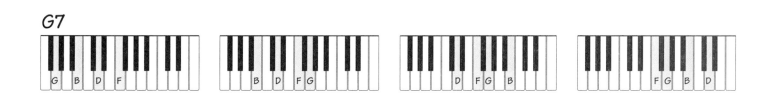

A♭7

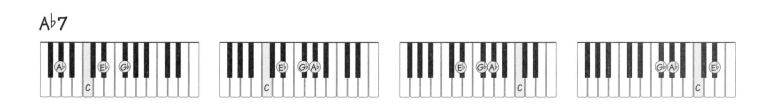

Root	1st Inversion	2nd Inversion	3rd Inversion

Am7

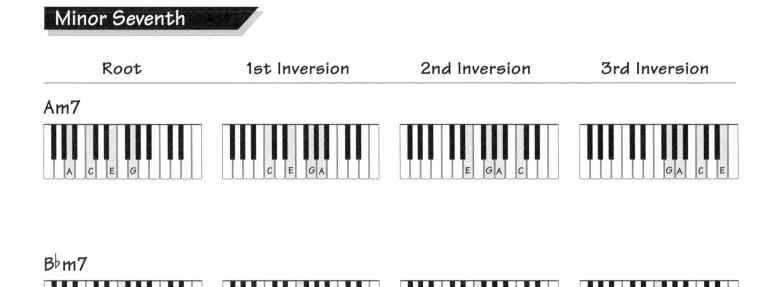

B♭m7

Bm7

Cm7

C♯m7/D♭m7

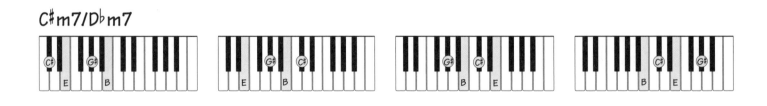

Dm7

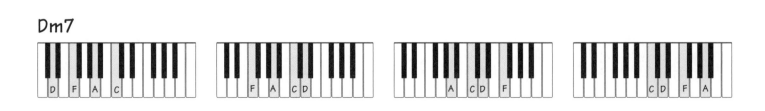

Root	1st Inversion	2nd Inversion	3rd Inversion

E♭m7

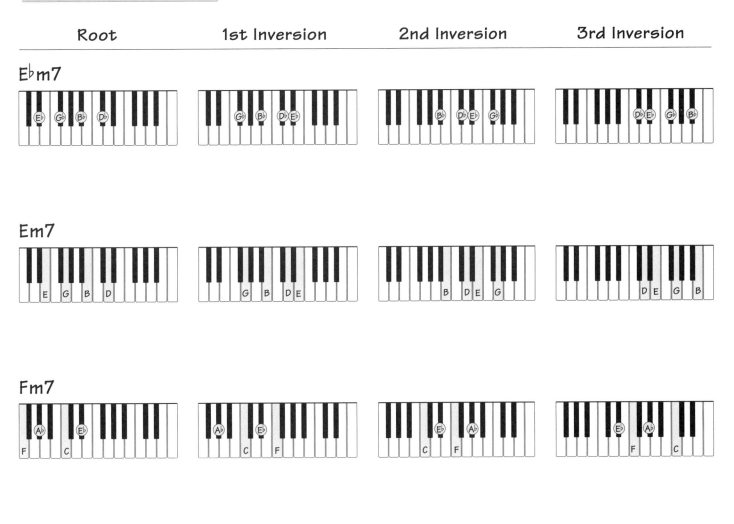

Em7

Fm7

F#m7/G♭m7

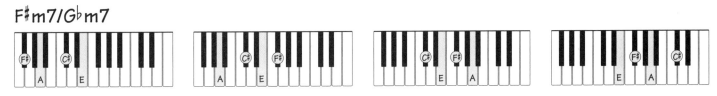

Gm7

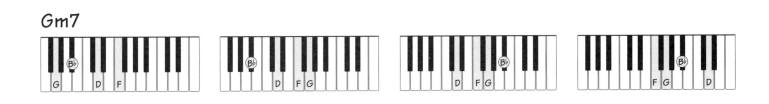

A♭m7

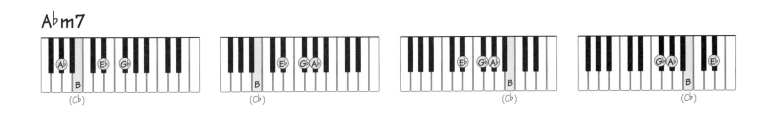

Major Seventh

	Root	1st Inversion	2nd Inversion	3rd Inversion

Amaj7

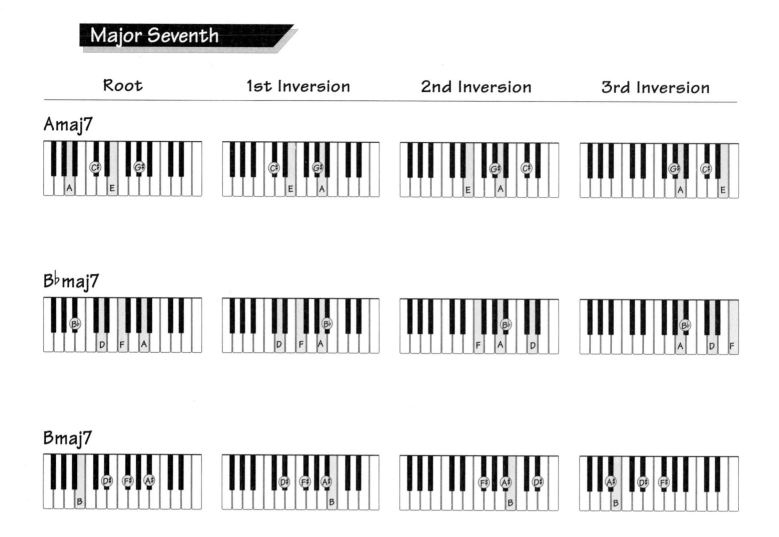

B♭maj7

Bmaj7

Cmaj7

C♯maj7/D♭maj7

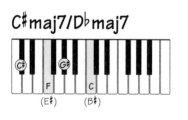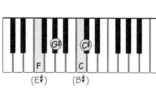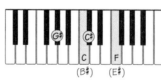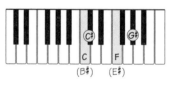

Dmaj7

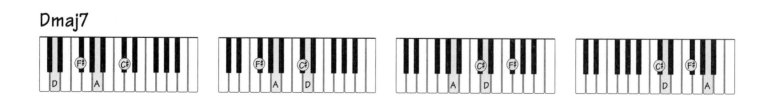

	Root	1st Inversion	2nd Inversion	3rd Inversion

E♭maj7

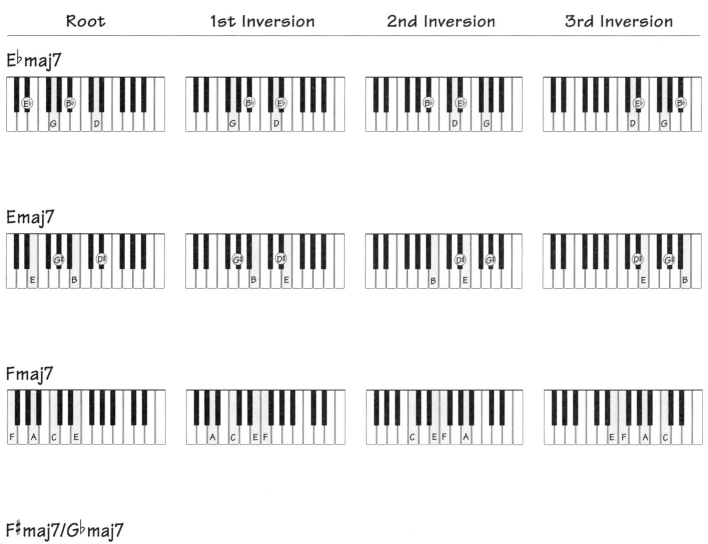

Emaj7

Fmaj7

F♯maj7/G♭maj7

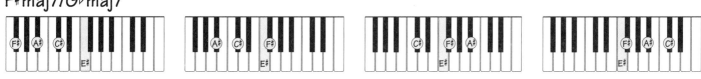

Gmaj7

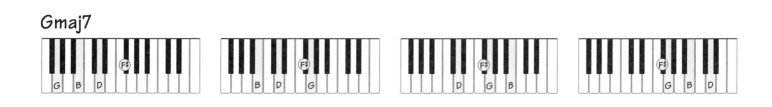

A♭maj7

	Root	1st Inversion	2nd Inversion	3rd Inversion

A7♯5

B♭7♯5

B7♯5

C7♯5

C♯7♯5/D♭7♯5

D7♯5

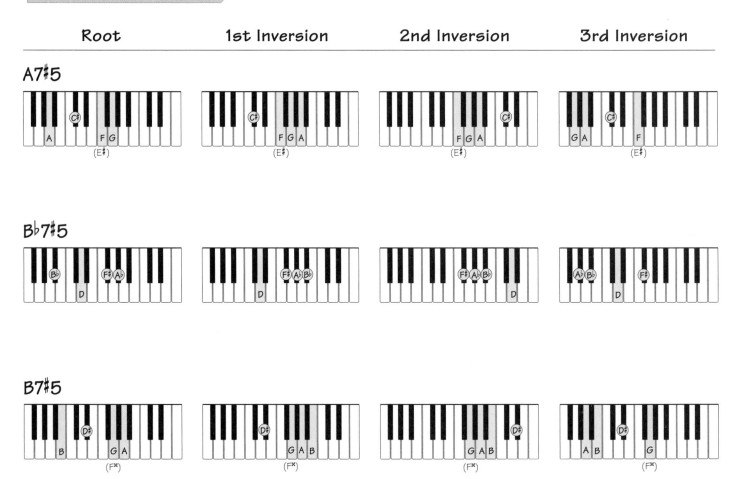
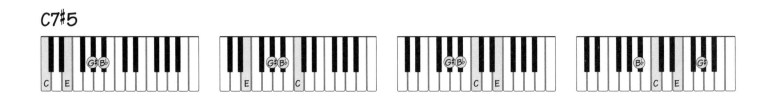
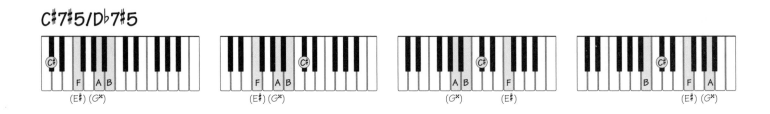
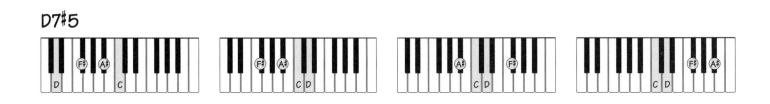

Root	1st Inversion	2nd Inversion	3rd Inversion

E♭7♯5
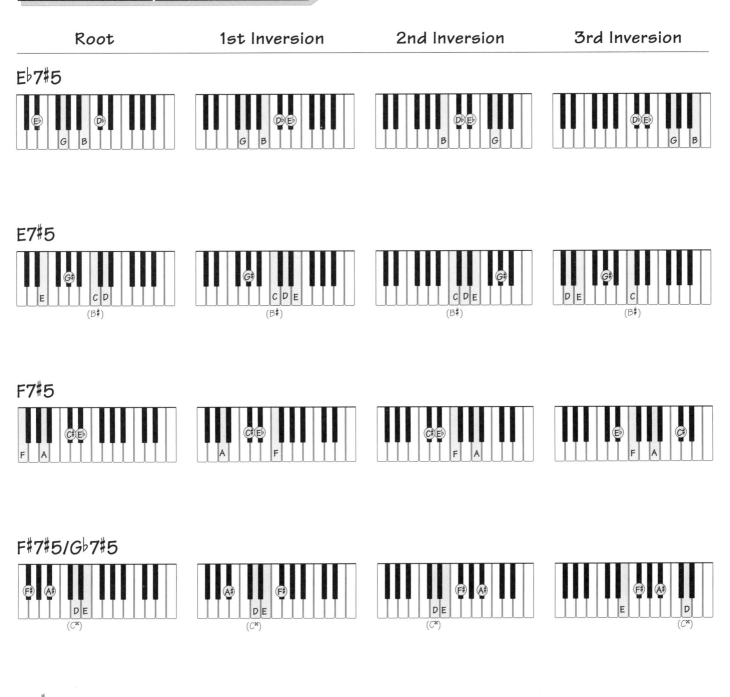

E7♯5

F7♯5

F♯7♯5/G♭7♯5
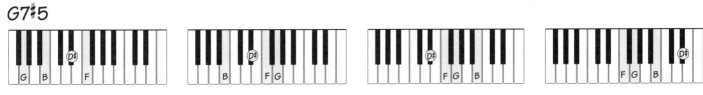

G7♯5

A♭7♯5
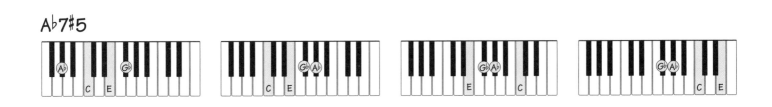

Diminished Seventh

Root	1st Inversion	2nd Inversion	3rd Inversion

Adim7

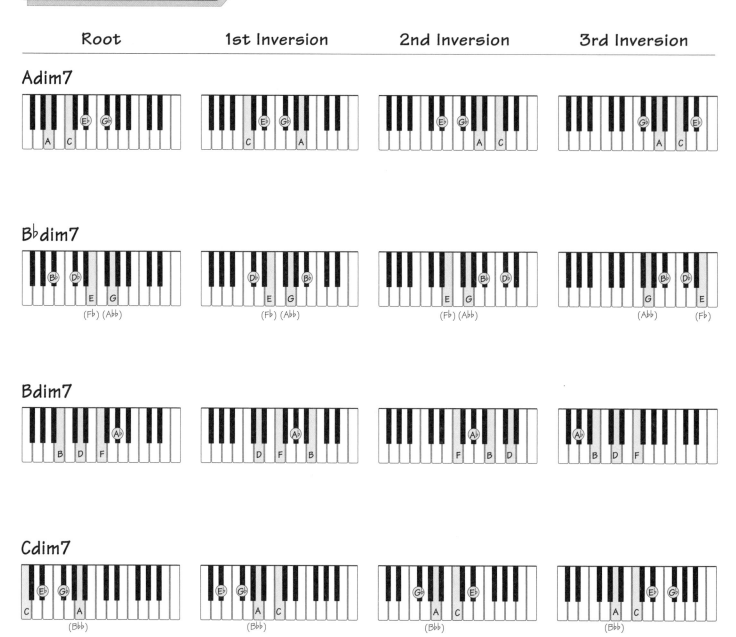

B♭dim7

Bdim7

Cdim7

C#dim7/D♭dim7

Ddim7

Diminished Seventh (cont.)

Root	1st Inversion	2nd Inversion	3rd Inversion

E♭dim7

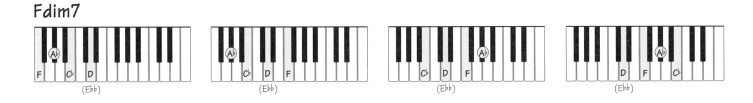

Edim7

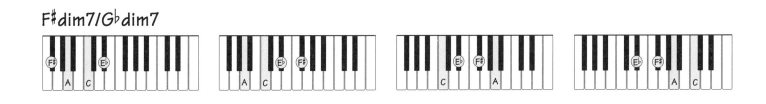

Fdim7

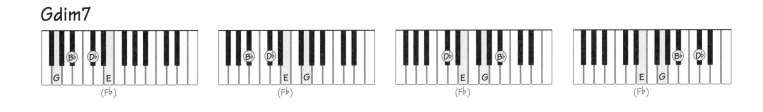

F♯dim7/G♭dim7

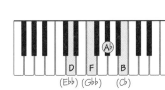

Gdim7

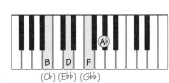

A♭dim7

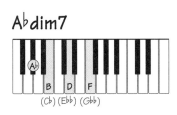
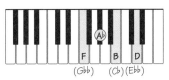

Root	1st Inversion	2nd Inversion	3rd Inversion

A7♭5

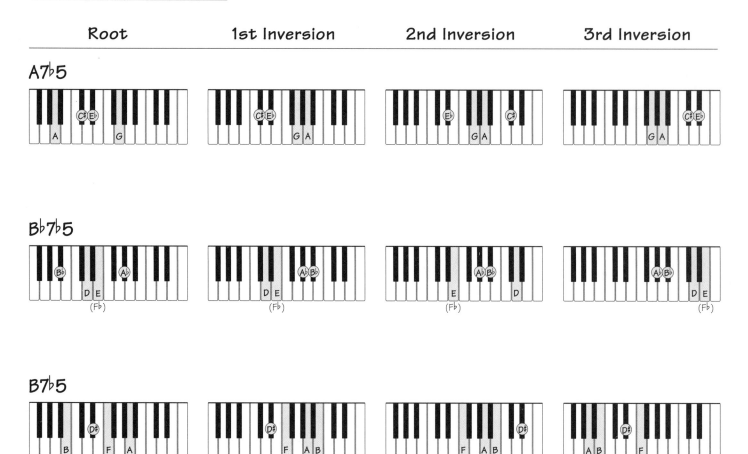

B♭7♭5

B7♭5

C7♭5

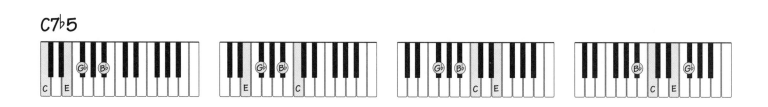

C#7♭5/D♭7♭5

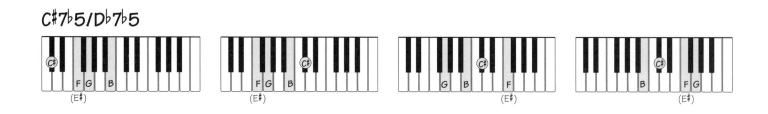

D7♭5

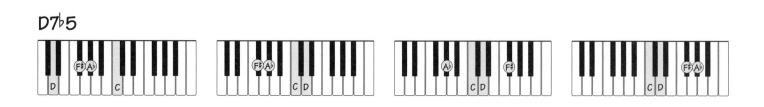

Root	1st Inversion	2nd Inversion	3rd Inversion

E♭7♭5

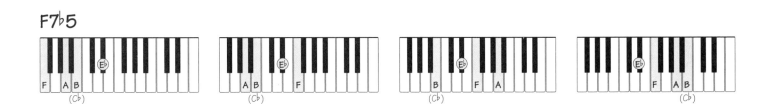

E7♭5

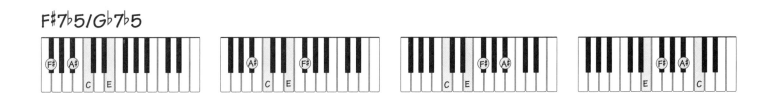

F7♭5

F#7♭5/G♭7♭5

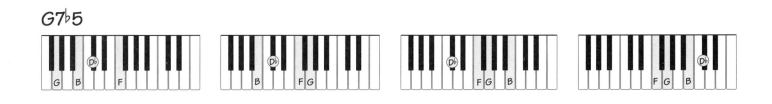

G7♭5

A♭7♭5

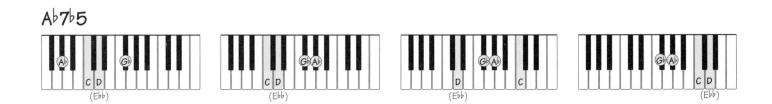

Root	1st Inversion	2nd Inversion	3rd Inversion

Am7♭5

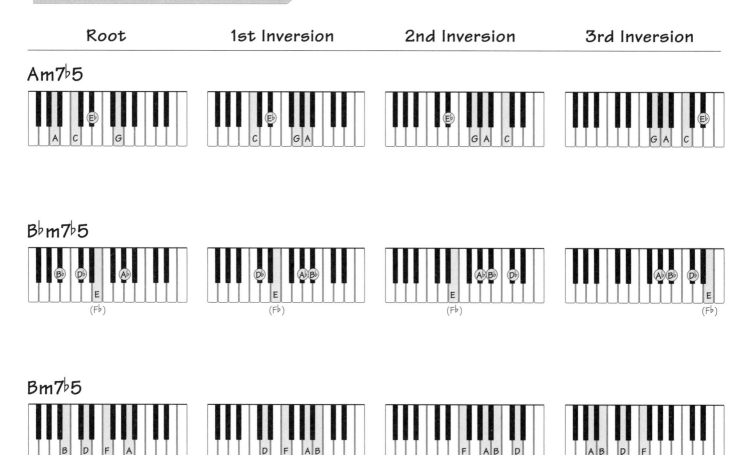

B♭m7♭5

Bm7♭5

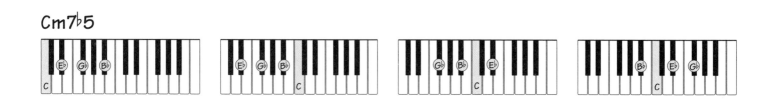

Cm7♭5

C♯m7♭5/D♭m7♭5

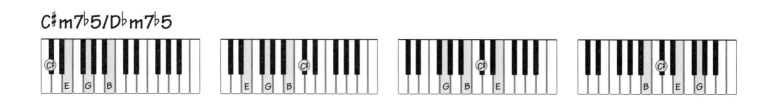

Dm7♭5

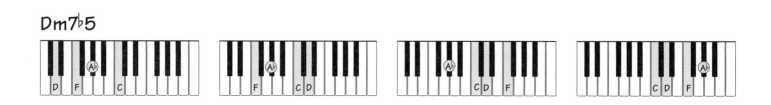

Root	1st Inversion	2nd Inversion	3rd Inversion

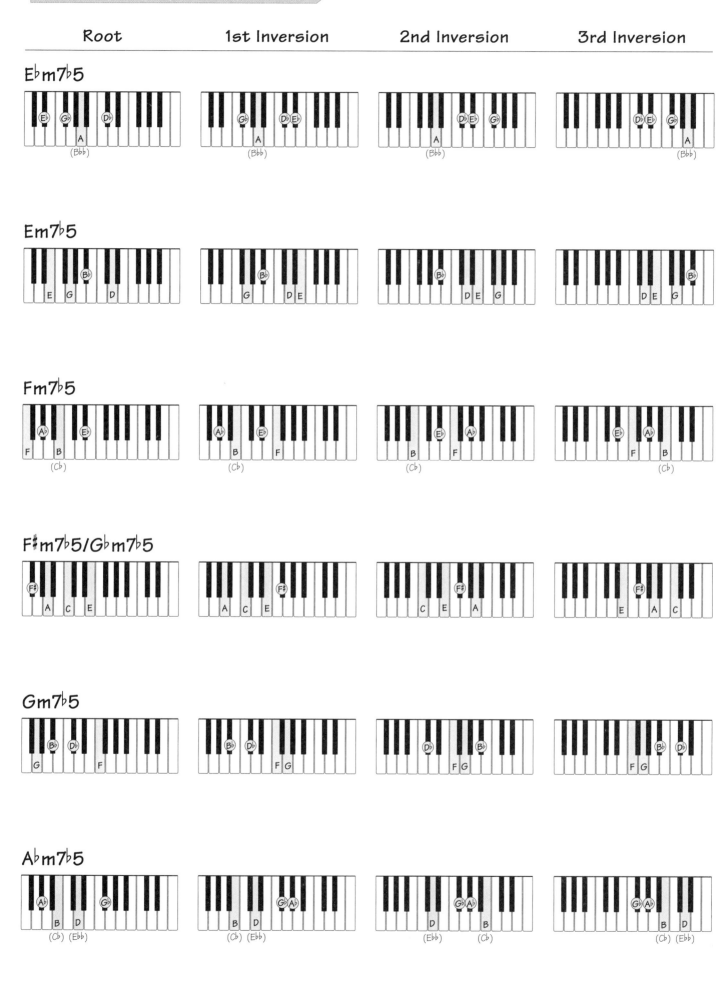

Sixth, Added Ninth

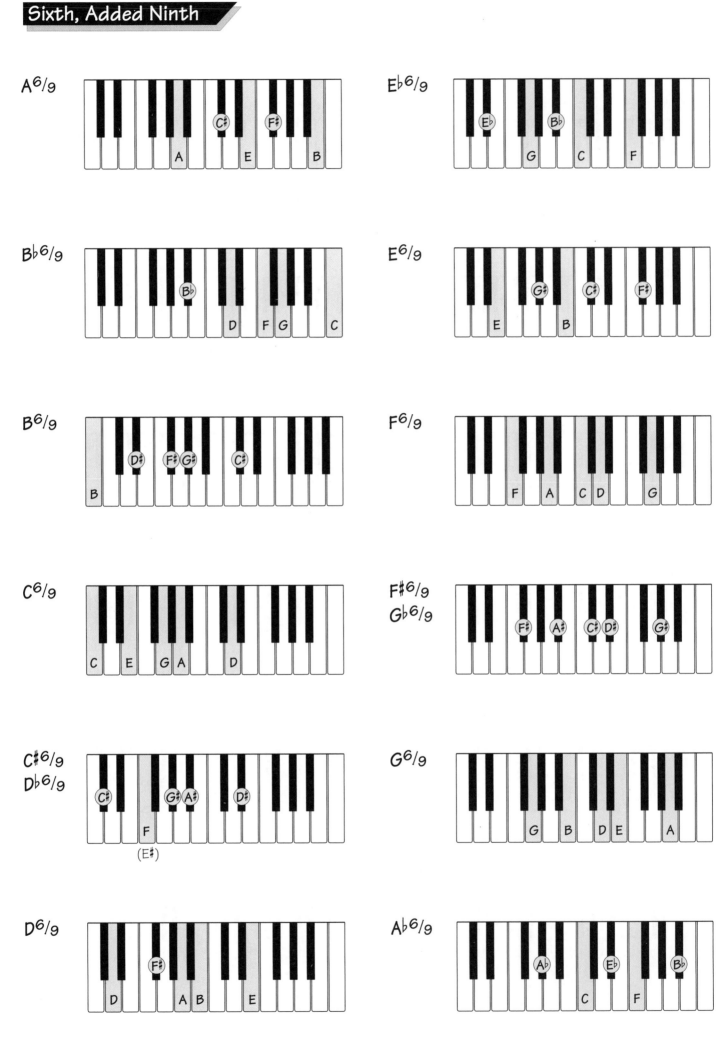

Seventh, Sharp Ninth

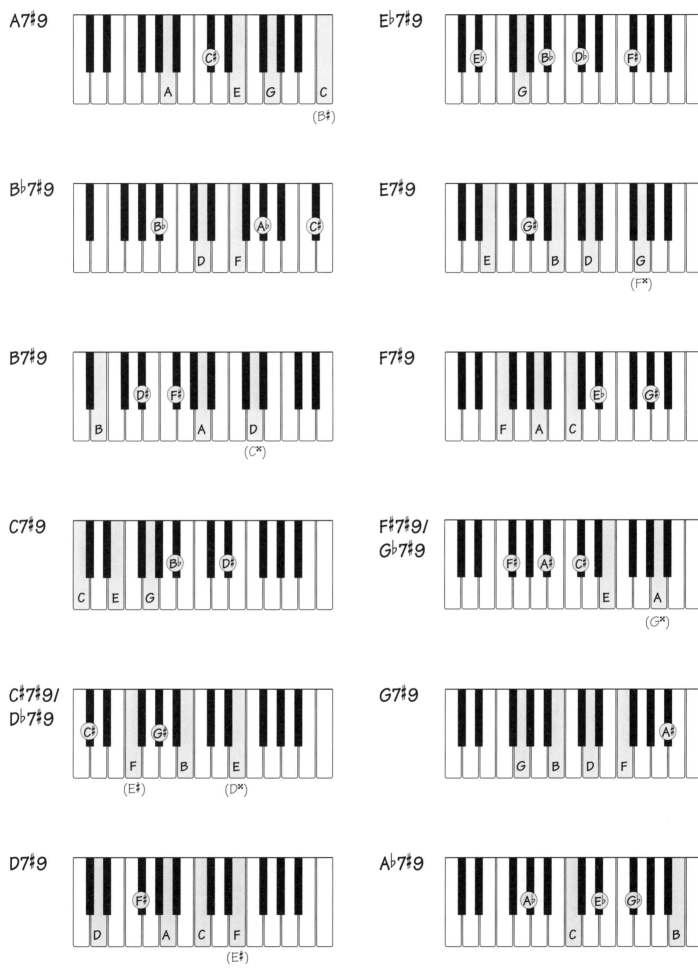

Seventh, Flat Ninth

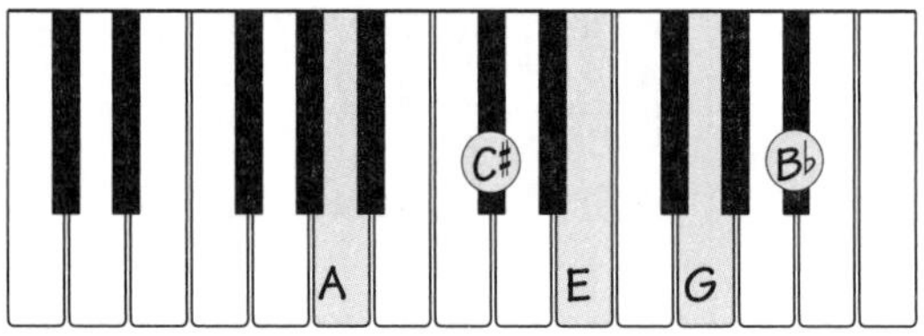

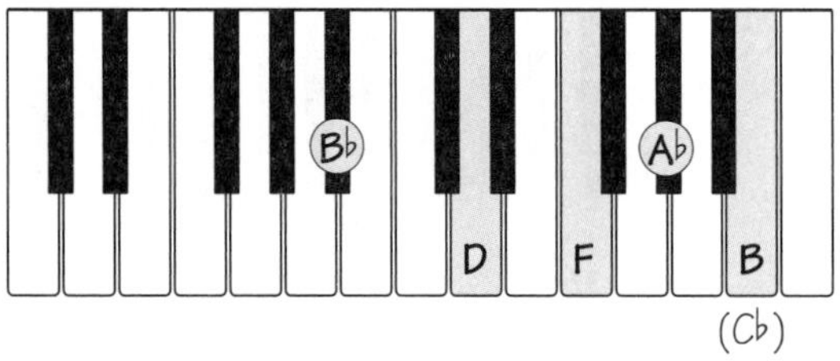

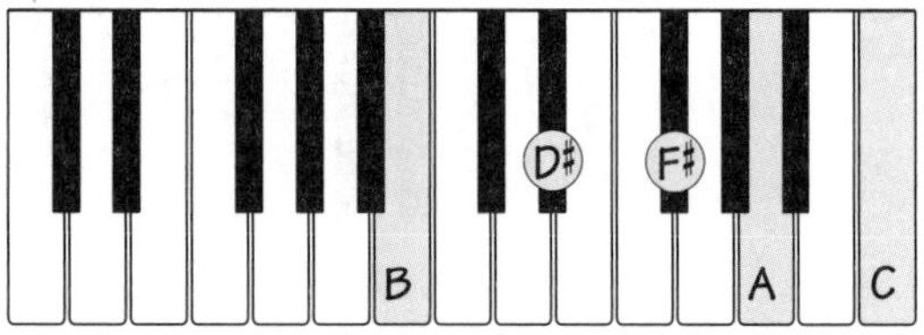

A7♭9

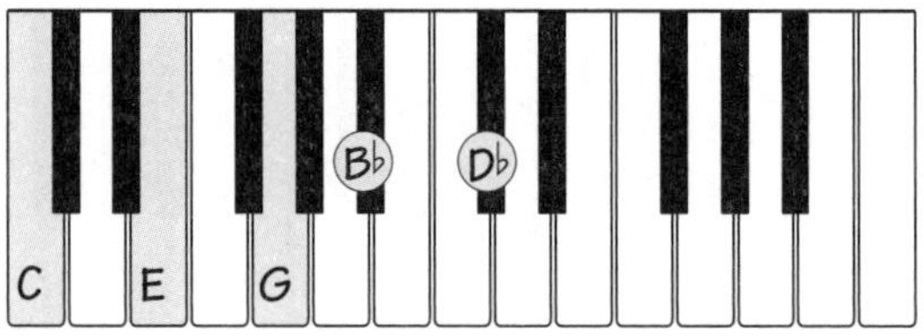

E♭7♭9

(F♭)

B♭7♭9

(C♭)

E7♭9

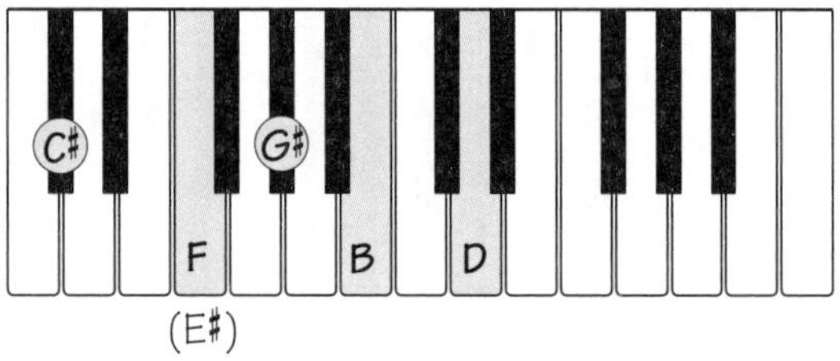

B7♭9

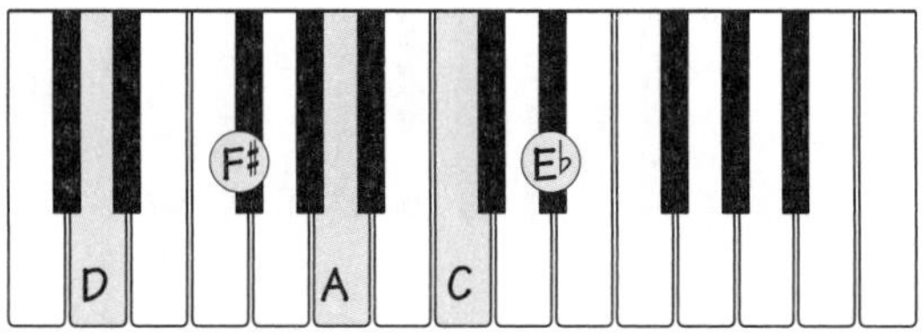

F7♭9

C7♭9

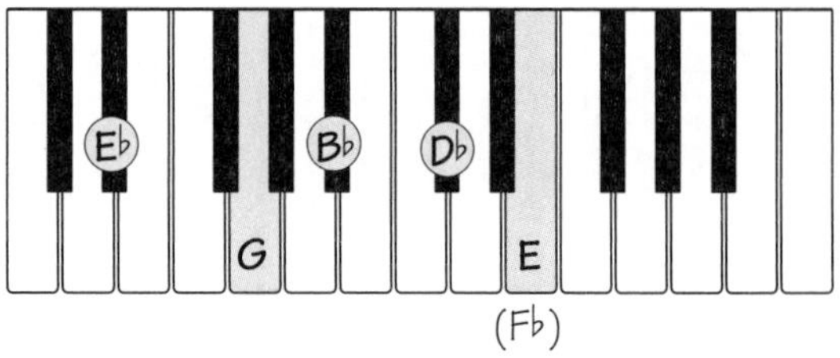

F#7♭9/
G♭7♭9

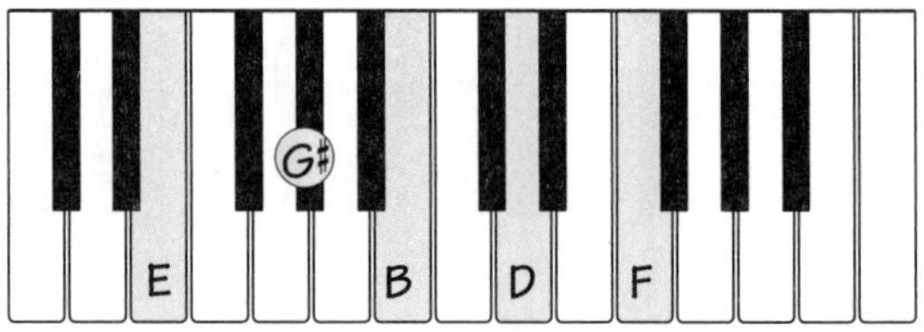

C#7♭9/
D♭7♭9

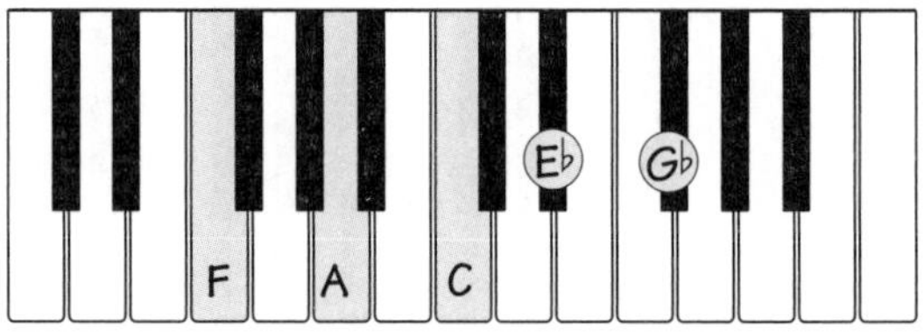

(E#)

G7♭9

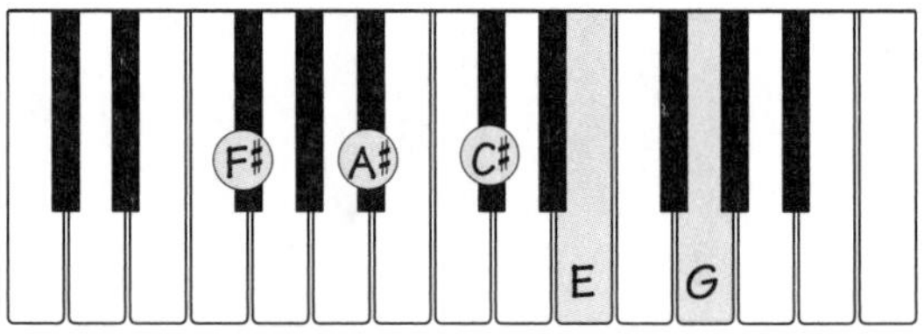

D7♭9

A♭7♭9

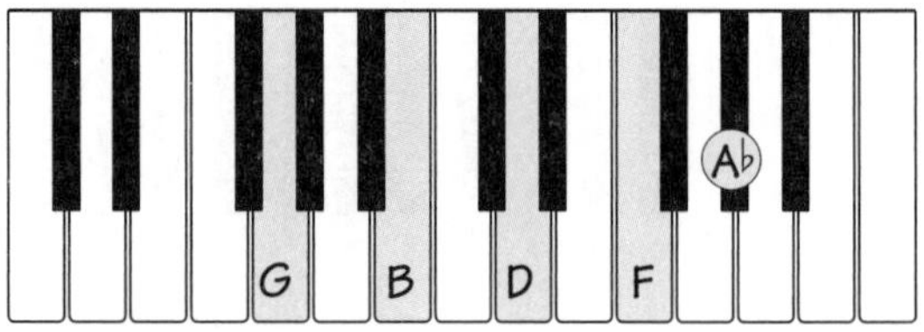

(B♭♭)

44

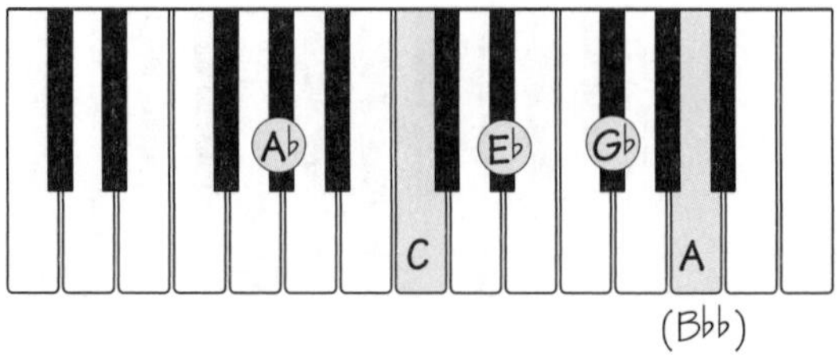

Ninth

A9

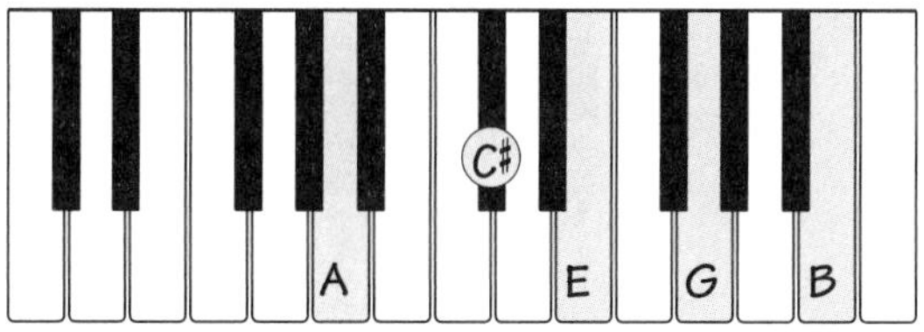

Bb9

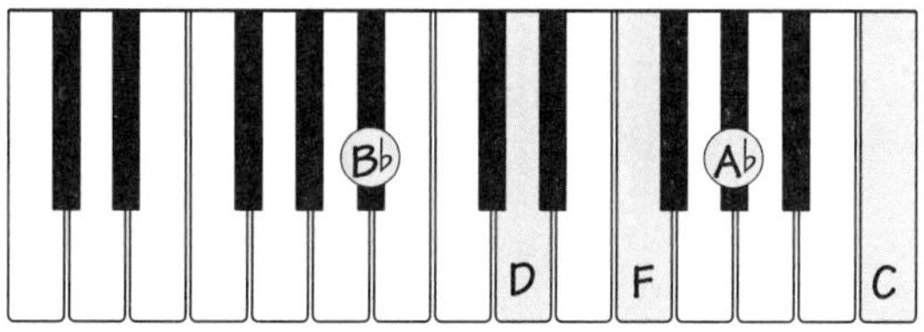

B9

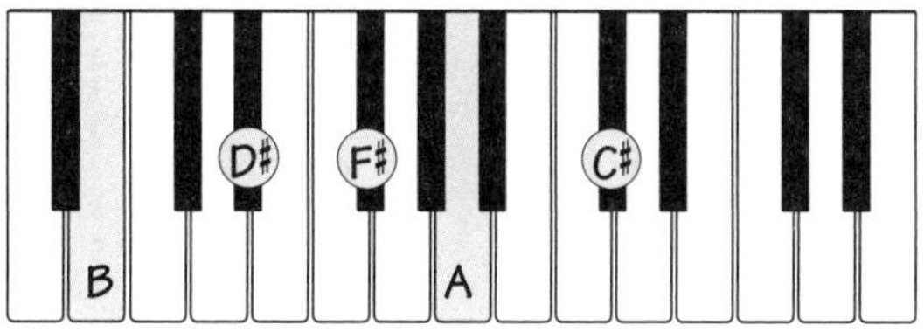

C9

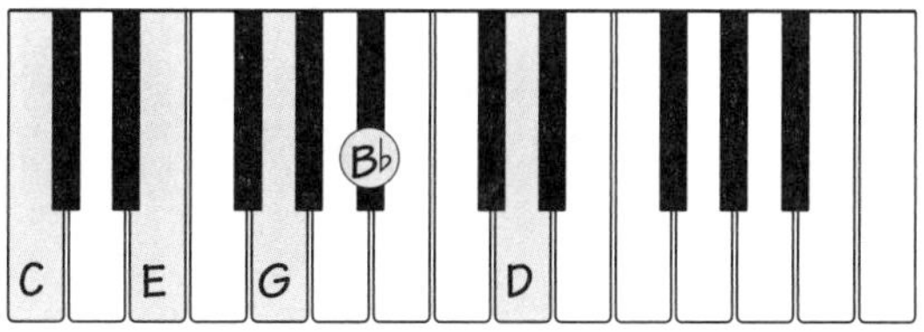

C#9/
D9

(E#)

D9

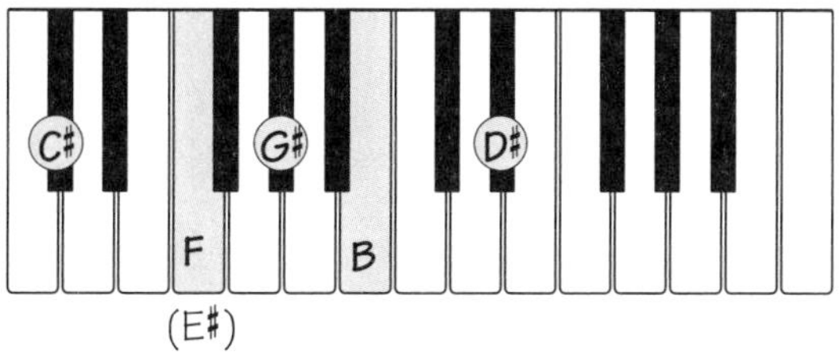

Eb9

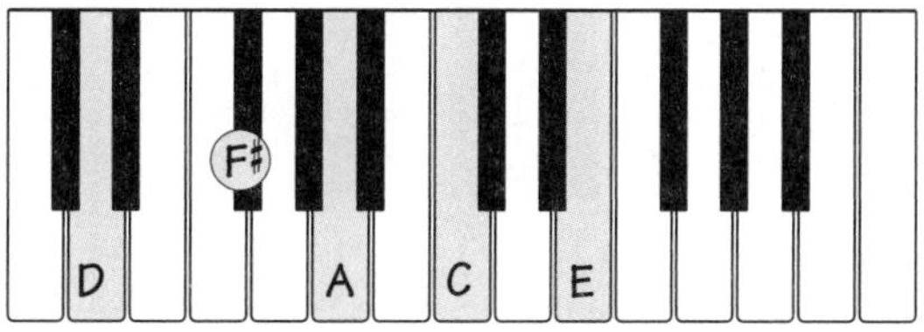

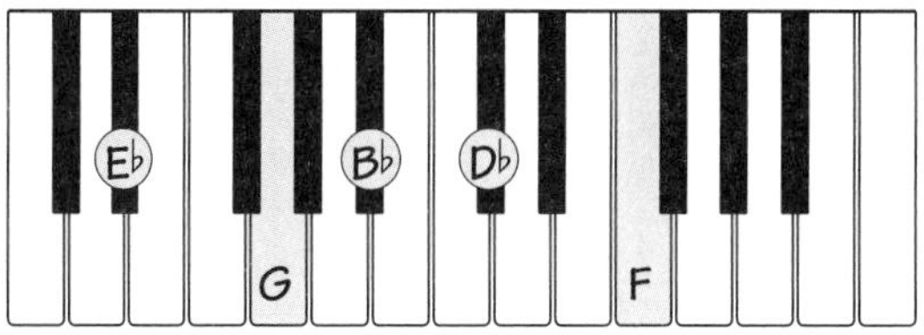

E9

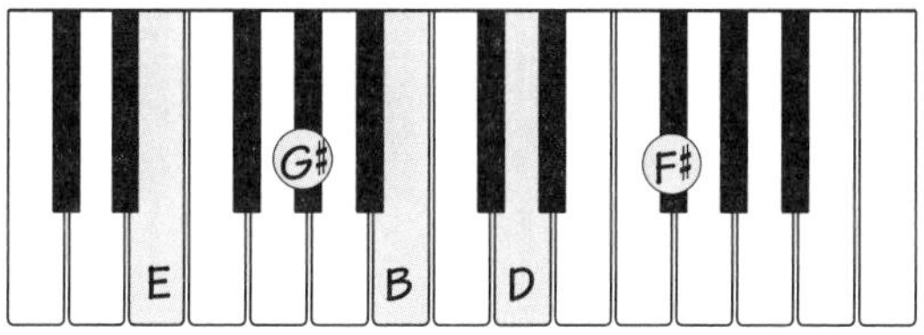

F9

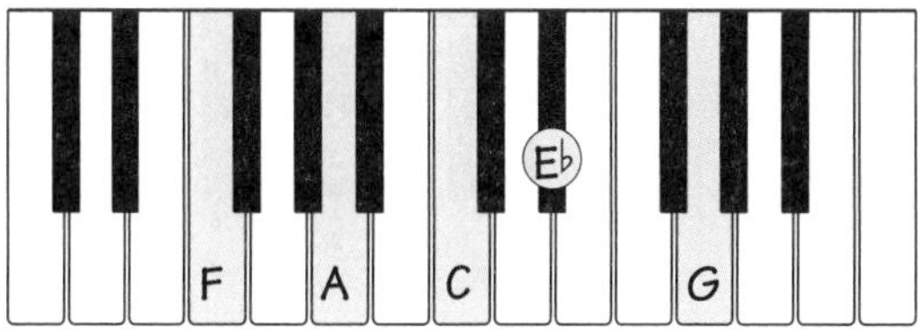

F#9/
Gb9

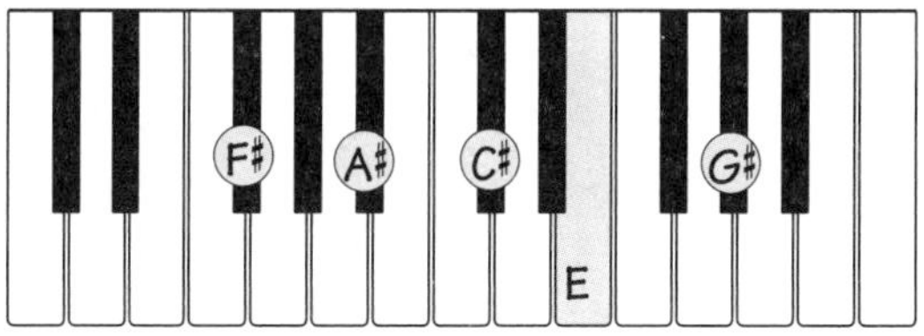

G9

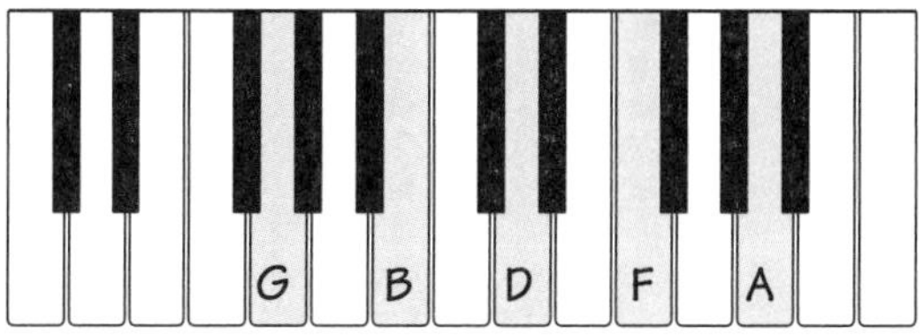

Ab9

45

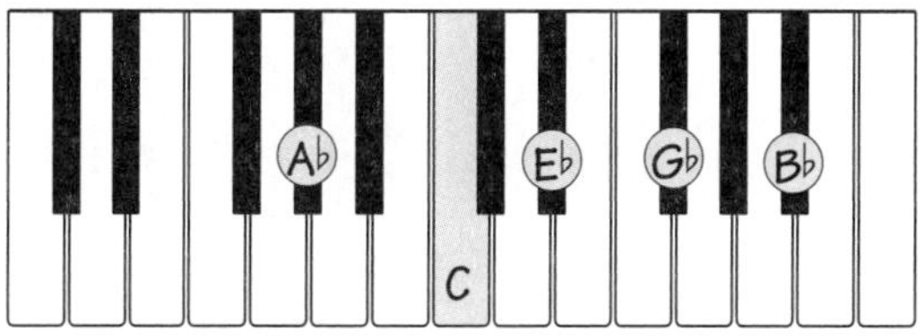

Minor Ninth

Am9

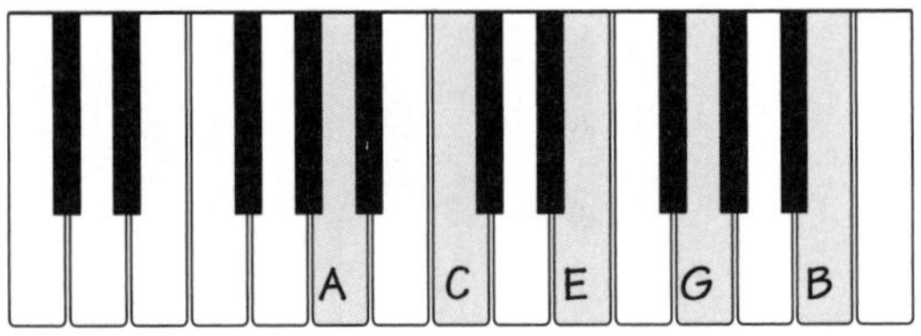

B♭m9

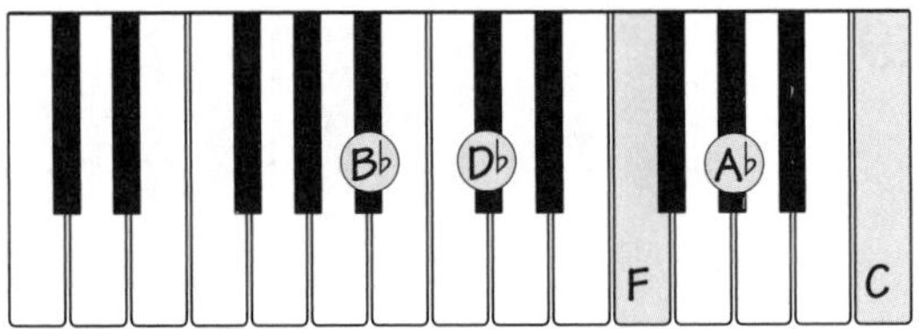

Bm9

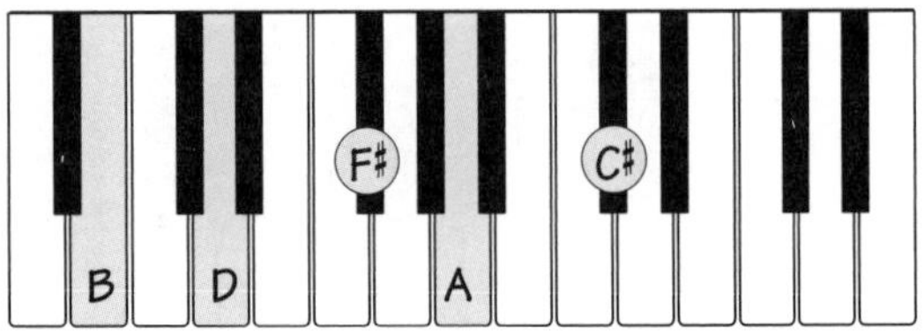

Cm9

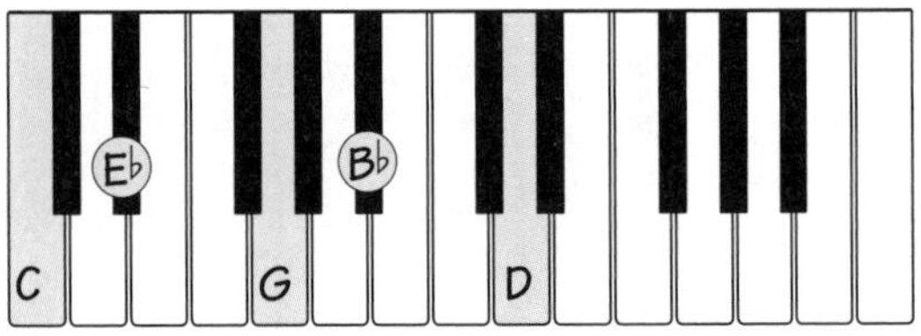

C#m9/
D♭m9

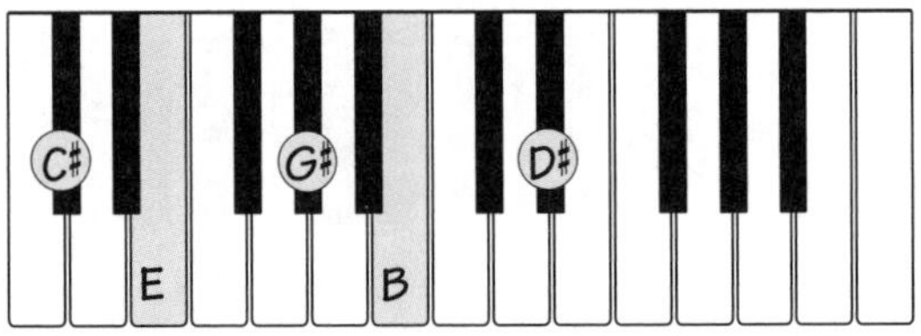

Dm9

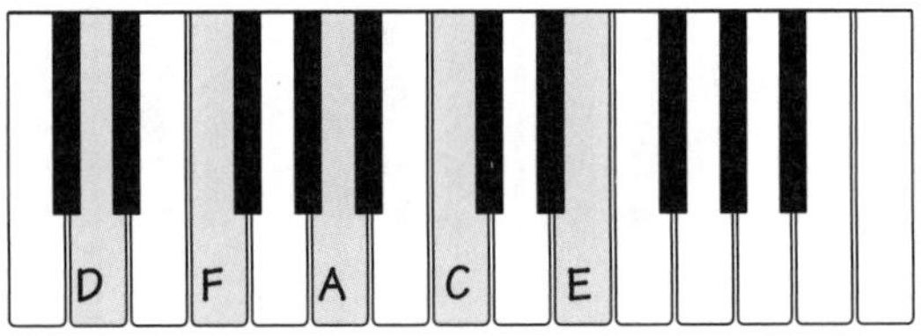

E♭m9

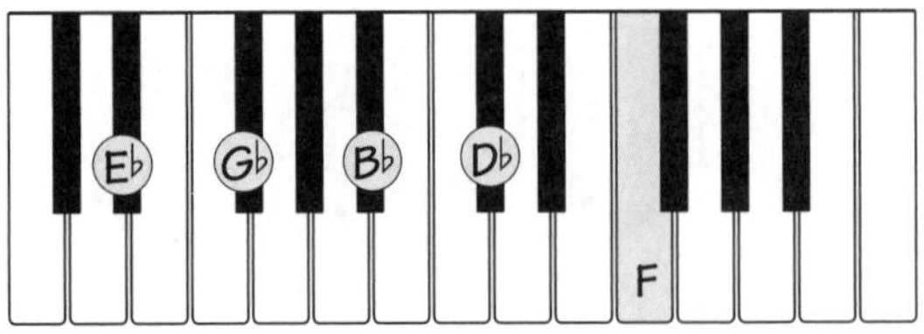

Em9

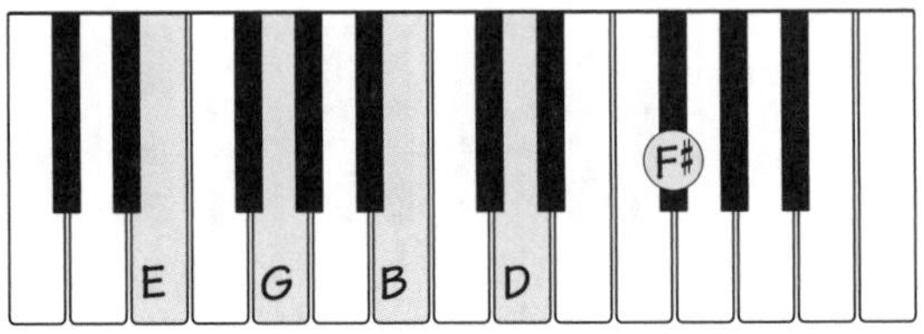

Fm9

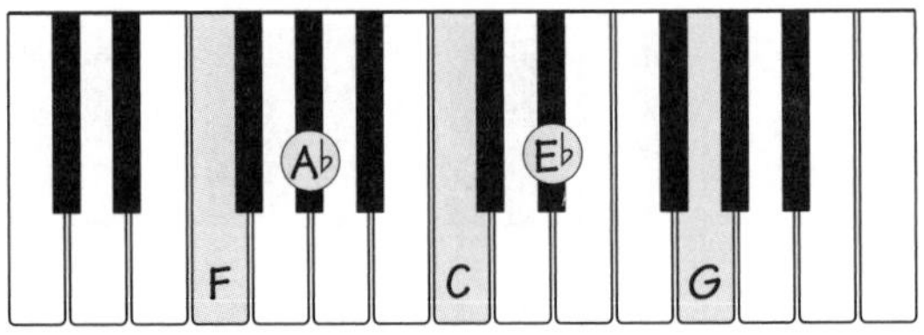

F#m9/
G♭m9

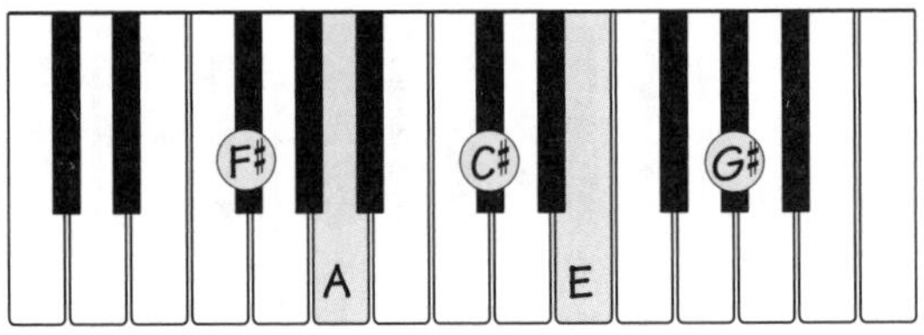

Gm9

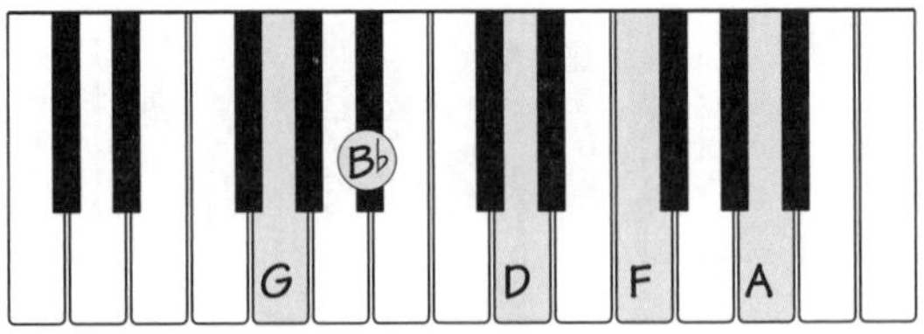

A♭m9

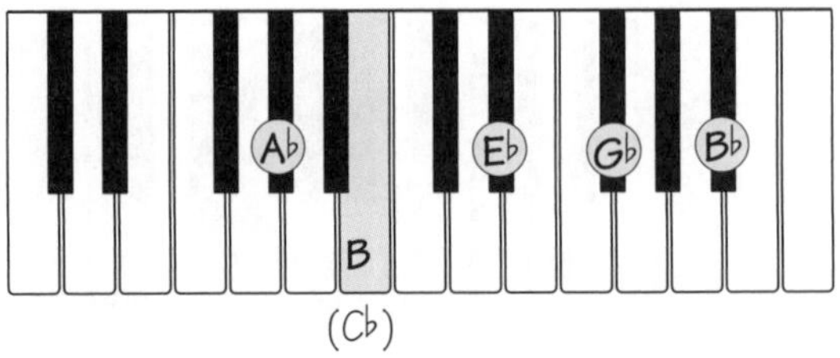

Eleventh

A11

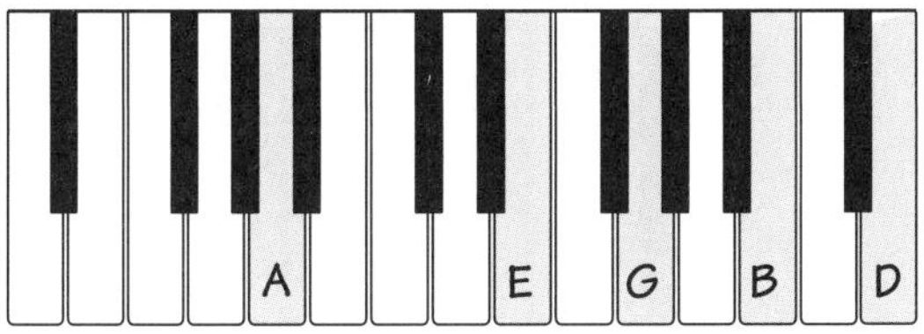

Bb11

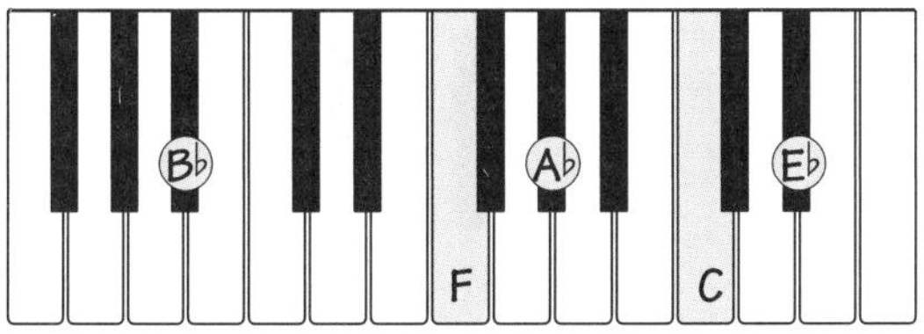

B11

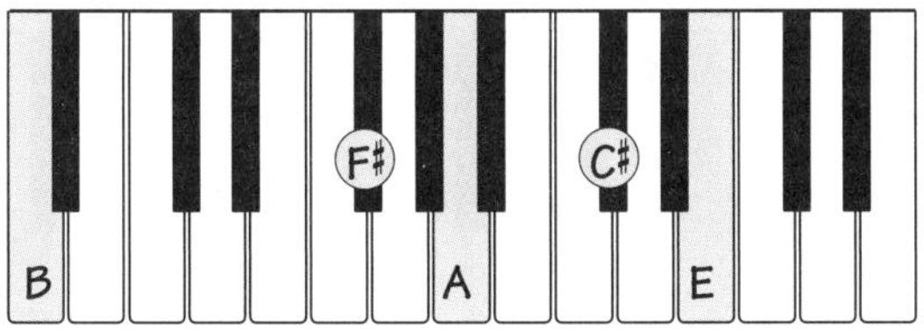

C11

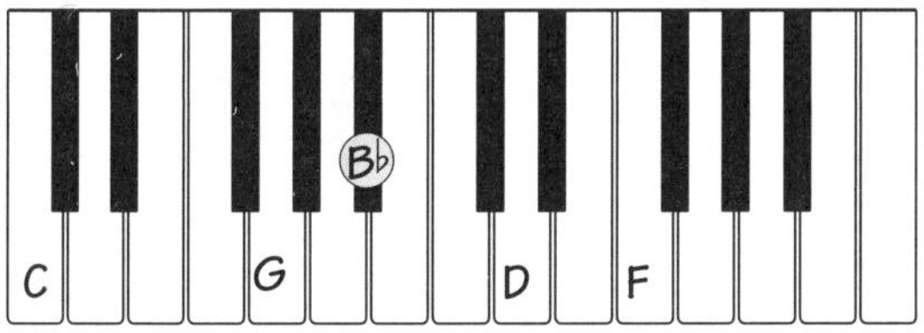

C#11/
Db11

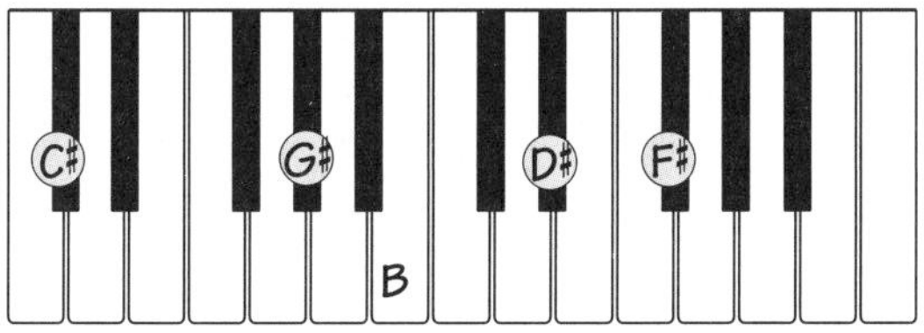

D11

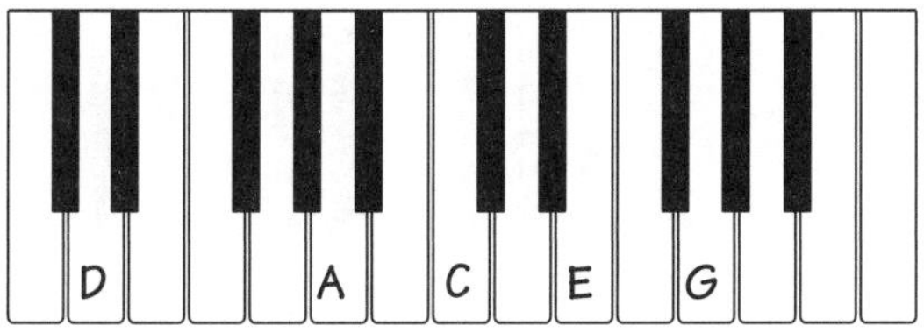

Eb11

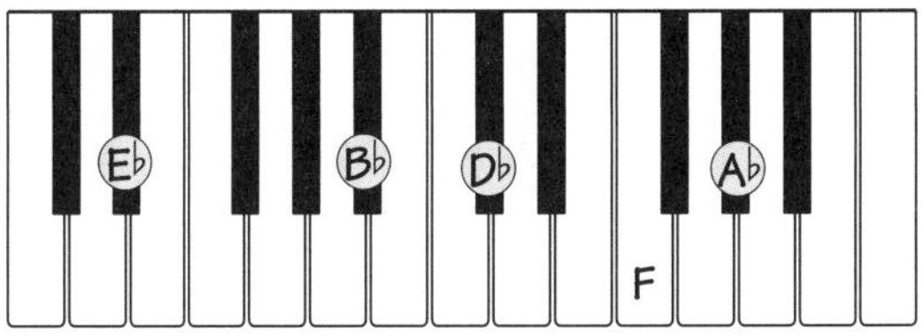

E11

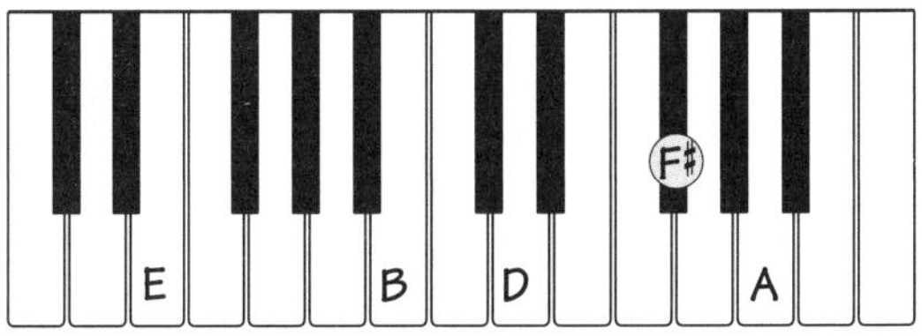

F11

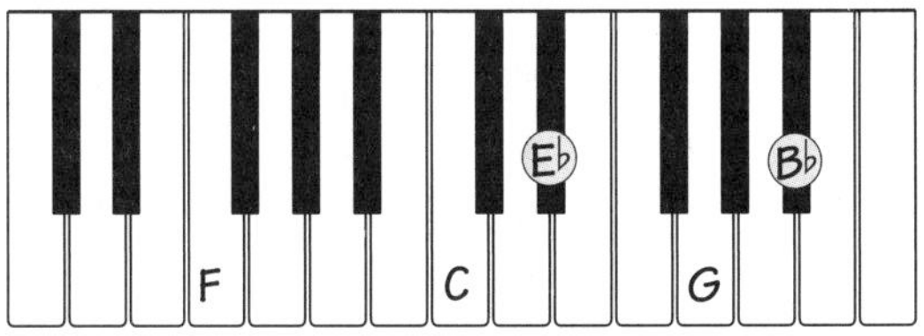

F#11/
Gb11

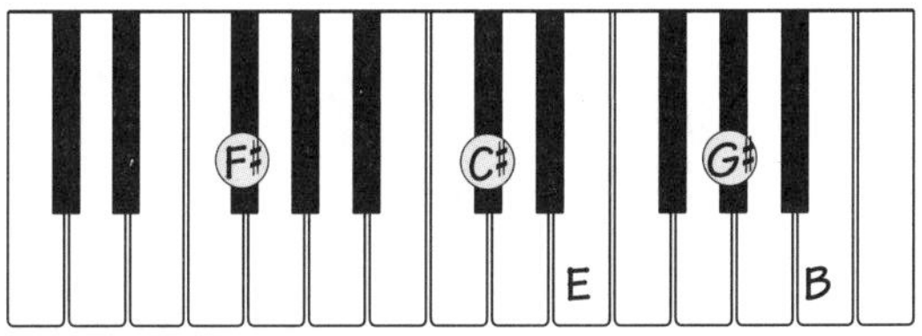

G11

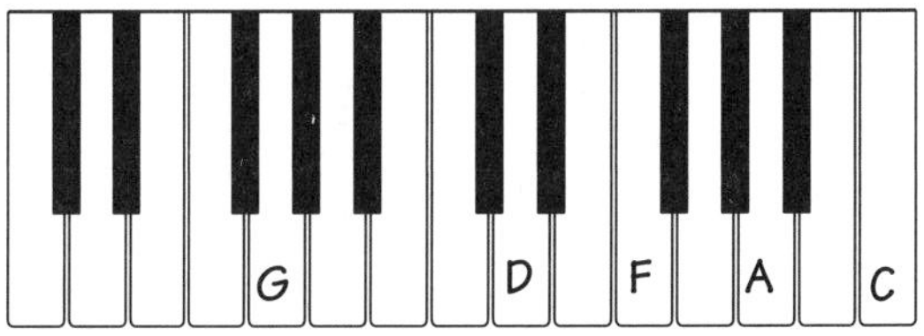

Ab11

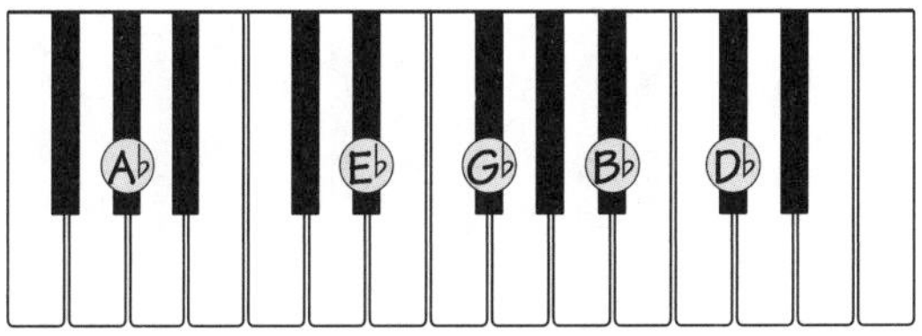

Minor Eleventh

Am11

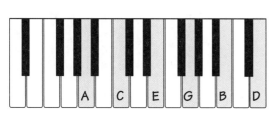

B♭m11

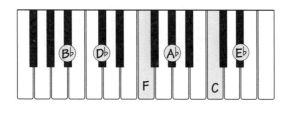

Bm11

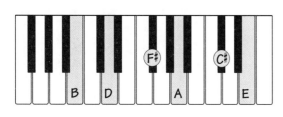

Cm11

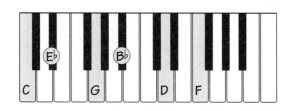

C#m11/
D♭m11

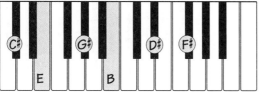

Dm11

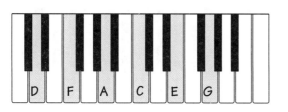

E♭m11

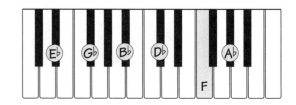

Em11

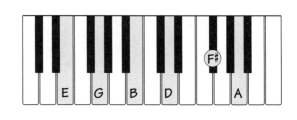

Fm11

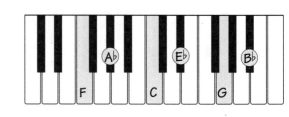

F#m11/
G♭m11

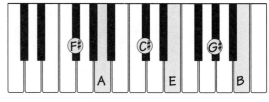

Gm11

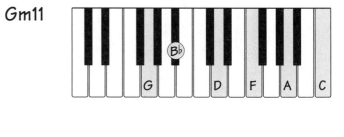

A♭m11

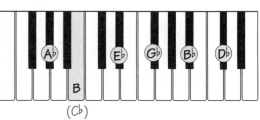

Thirteenth

A13

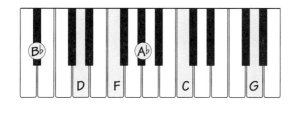

Eb13

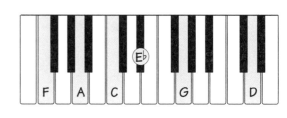

Bb13

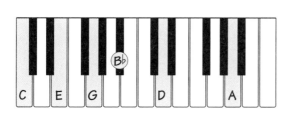

E13

B13

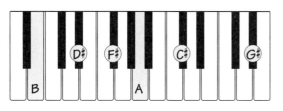

F13

C13

F#13/
Gb13

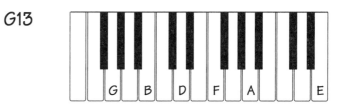

C#13/
Db13

(E#)

G13

D13

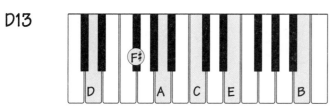

Ab13

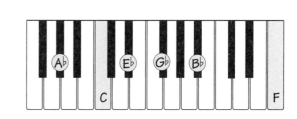

BUILDING SCALES

Scale (from L. *scala*, ladder): a progression of notes in a specific order. Also, the "skin" on a fish!

Scales are very important to know, especially when it comes to playing a solo. This section is an easy reference for constructing, locating and playing the essential scales on your keyboard. By the end of this section, you can use scales to improvise over the "Jam Session" on the audio.

One step at a time...

Each scale has a specific pattern of whole steps, half steps, and sometimes one and a half steps. To build a scale, simply choose a root note and apply a pattern. We've given you two ways to build (or "spell") each scale:

1. Note Names   (ex. A—B—C—D—E—F—G—A)

The most common way to spell a scale is by its note names. The note names for each scale are relative to the root note. Of course, the note names of a scale will vary (natural, sharp or flat) depending on the pattern of steps used to create that scale.

Here's a comparison of E major and E minor. Notice how the spelling is different for the third, sixth and seventh tones:

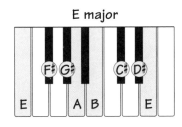
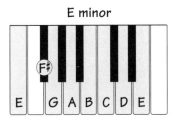

2. Step Pattern   (ex. W—H—W—W—H—W+H—H)

This pattern tells you how many steps to move from one scale tone to the next, using abbreviations for whole step (W), half step (H) and 1 1/2 steps (W+H). Simply start on any root note and move up accordingly.

☞ REMEMBER: Sharps and flats are unavoidable with scales (except for C major and A minor). So, don't be alarmed if a particular step causes you to play one.

Here's an example of building a major scale on the root note A, using a step pattern:

Step pattern = W—W—H—W—W—W—H

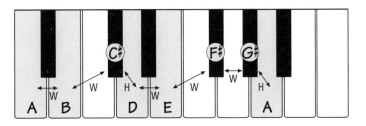

Rockin' result = A—B—C#—D—E—F#—G#—A

Pick a hand, any hand...

You'll notice that each of the scale patterns in this book are shown in diagrams rather than notation. This is so you can learn to play them with either the right or left hand (or both at the same time!)

Speakin' of fingering...

When playing scales, it's extremely important to use correct fingering. Please make it a habit to learn the correct fingering at the same time you learn each scale pattern.

Notice that the fingering differs according to the direction you are playing the scale—up or down.

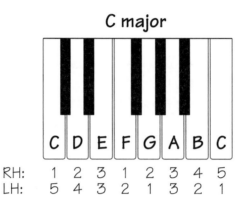

Correct fingering will enable you to play faster, smoother, and just plain better!

☞ PRACTICE TIP: Make sure you play each scale forward and then backward. And. as always, start out slow and gradually build up speed as you build up confidence.

That's about all...good luck and have fun!

MAJOR

The most common scale used in music is the **major** scale, so learn it well! It consists of eight consecutive notes ascending or descending.

Step pattern: W—W—H—W—W—W—H

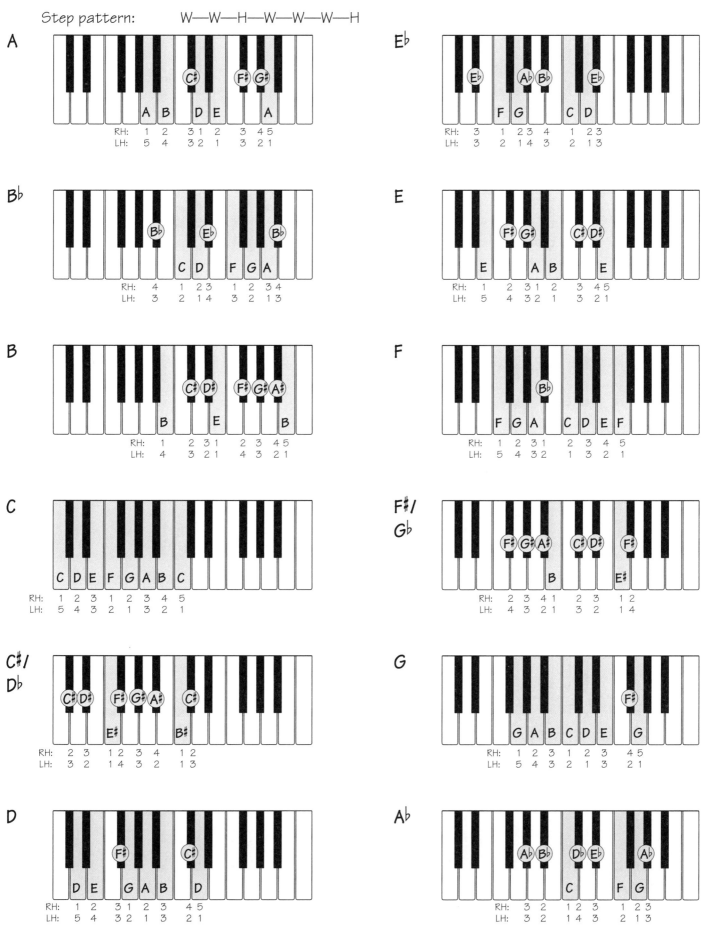

MINOR

This scale is used in nearly all styles of Western music. It's sometimes referred to as the "pure minor," "relative minor," or "Aeolian mode."

Step pattern: W—H—W—W—H—W—W

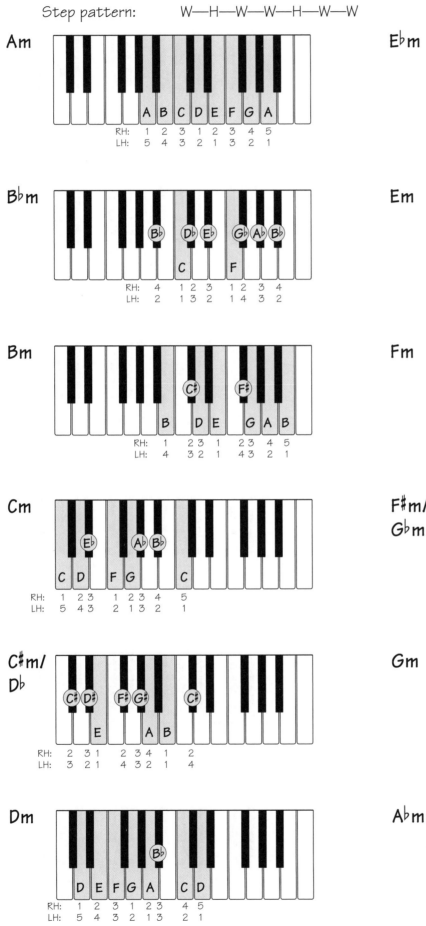

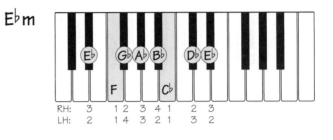

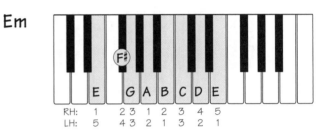

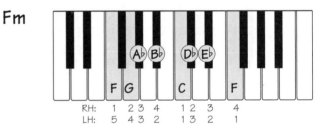

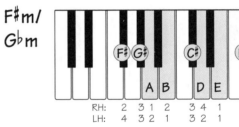
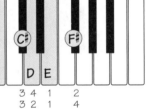

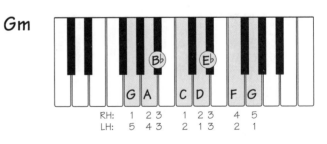

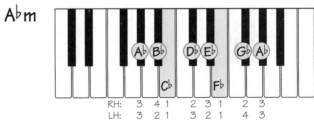

HARMONIC MINOR

This scale provides an alternative minor scale type and is very common in classical music.

Step pattern: W—H—W—W—H—W+H—H

Am
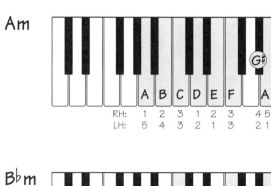

RH: 1 2 3 1 2 3 4 5
LH: 5 4 3 2 1 3 2 1

B♭m
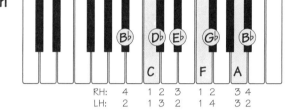

RH: 4 1 2 3 1 2 3 4
LH: 2 1 3 2 1 4 3 2

Bm
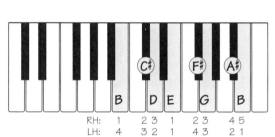

RH: 1 2 3 1 2 3 4 5
LH: 4 3 2 1 4 3 2 1

Cm
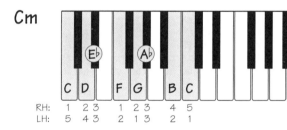

RH: 1 2 3 1 2 3 4 5
LH: 5 4 3 2 1 3 2 1

C♯m/ D♭m
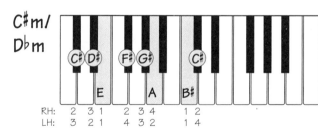

RH: 2 3 1 2 3 4 1 2
LH: 3 2 1 4 3 2 1 4

Dm
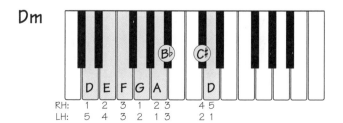

RH: 1 2 3 1 2 3 4 5
LH: 5 4 3 2 1 3 2 1

E♭m
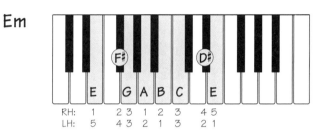

RH: 3 1 2 3 4 1 2 3
LH: 2 1 4 3 2 1 3 2

Em
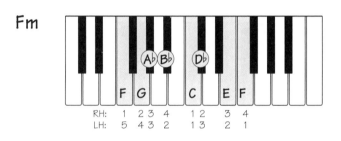

RH: 1 2 3 1 2 3 4 5
LH: 5 4 3 2 1 3 2 1

Fm
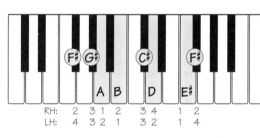

RH: 1 2 3 4 1 2 3 4
LH: 5 4 3 2 1 3 2 1

F♯m/ G♭m

RH: 2 3 1 2 3 4 1 2
LH: 4 3 2 1 3 2 1 4

Gm

RH: 1 2 3 1 2 3 4 5
LH: 5 4 3 2 1 3 2 1

A♭m
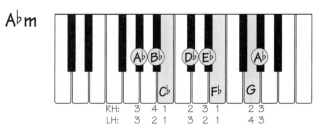

RH: 3 4 1 2 3 1 2 3
LH: 3 2 1 3 2 1 4 3

MELODIC MINOR

This scale can also be used over minor chords and is commonly referred to as the "jazz minor" scale.

Step pattern: W—H—W—W—W—W—H

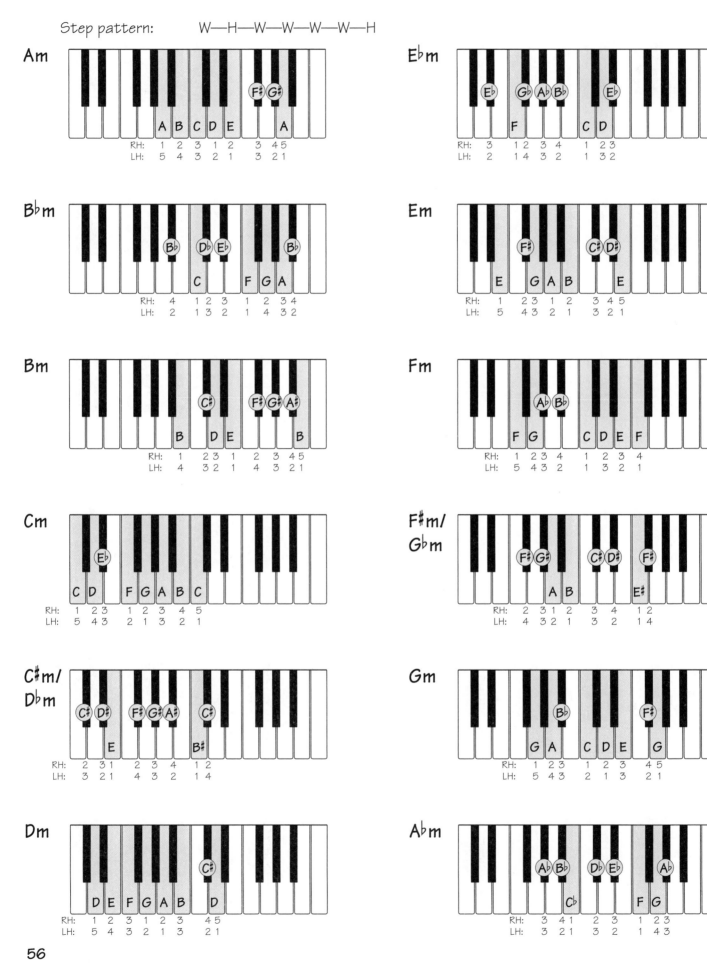

56

BLUES

The **blues** scale is common in jazz, rock, and (you guessed it!) blues music. It contains an added **blues note** (♭5) from the minor pentatonic scale but has only seven tones.

Step pattern: W+H—W—H—H—W+H—W

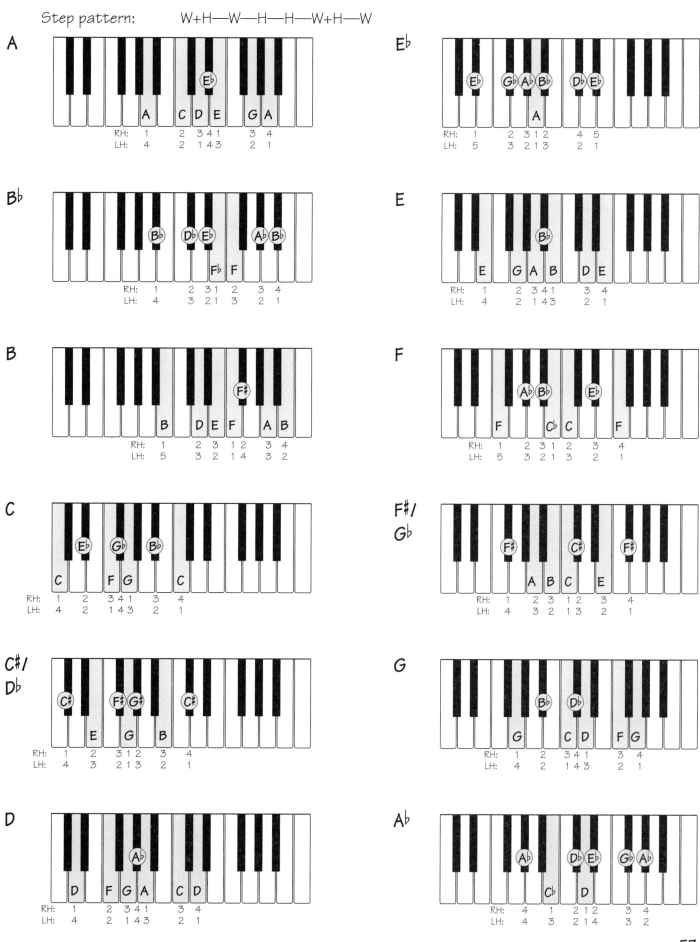

MODES

Modes are like scales—each uses a specific pattern of whole steps and half steps. The difference is that a mode is not related to the **key** of its root note. That is, a Dorian mode built on C is not in the key of C. The seven modes in common practice today are derived from the seven notes of the major scale:

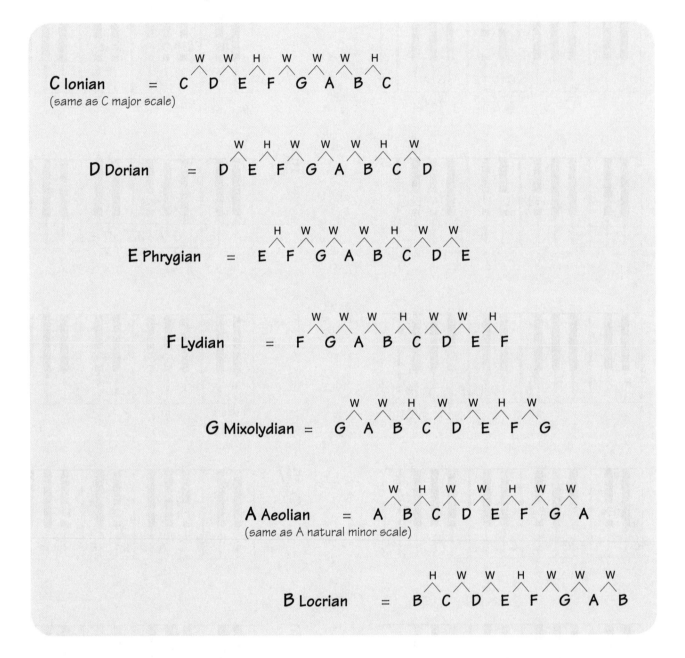

As you can see, each mode is actually a variation of the major scale. They differ only in the arrangement of the intervals.

The next page shows each mode on two different root notes. Once you understand it, try applying the patterns to each of the other ten root notes…

F   **G**

Ionian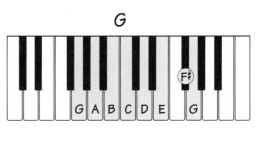

Dorian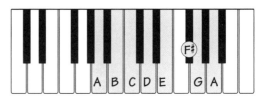

Phrygian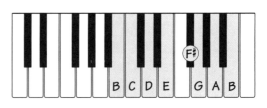

Lydian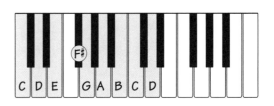

Mixolydian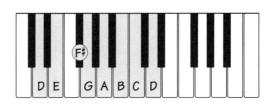

Aeolian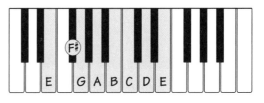

Locrian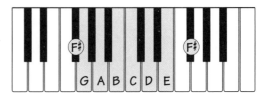

JAM SESSION
Time to charge admission...

Now it's time to use the chords and scales from this book and make some **actual music!** This section provides twenty chord progressions found in various music styles. Play along with the audio. You can either follow the chord symbols and play along, or use the suggested scales to practice improvising.

Either way, turn it up, and let's jam!

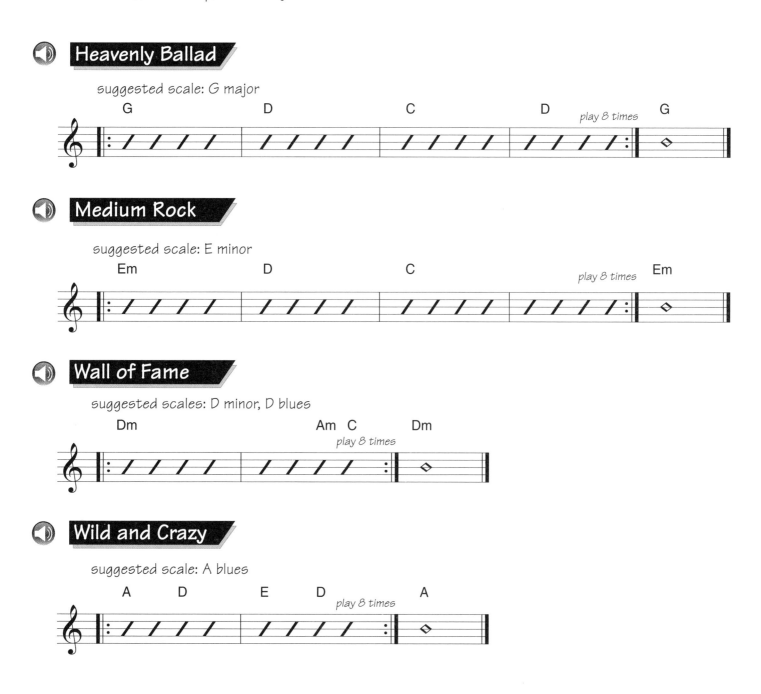

Heavenly Ballad

suggested scale: G major

G   D   C   D   *play 8 times*   G

Medium Rock

suggested scale: E minor

Em   D   C   *play 8 times*   Em

Wall of Fame

suggested scales: D minor, D blues

Dm   Am   C   Dm   *play 8 times*

Wild and Crazy

suggested scale: A blues

A   D   E   D   *play 8 times*   A

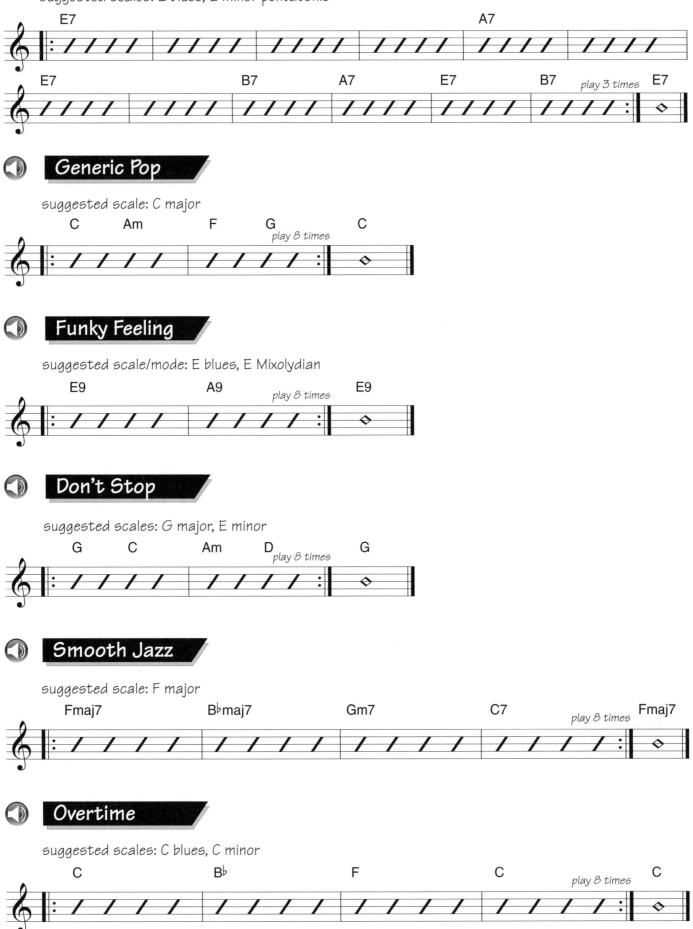

Full Deck Shuffle

suggested scales: E blues, E minor pentatonic

Generic Pop

suggested scale: C major

Funky Feeling

suggested scale/mode: E blues, E Mixolydian

Don't Stop

suggested scales: G major, E minor

Smooth Jazz

suggested scale: F major

Overtime

suggested scales: C blues, C minor

Nashville Dreamin'

suggested scale: C major

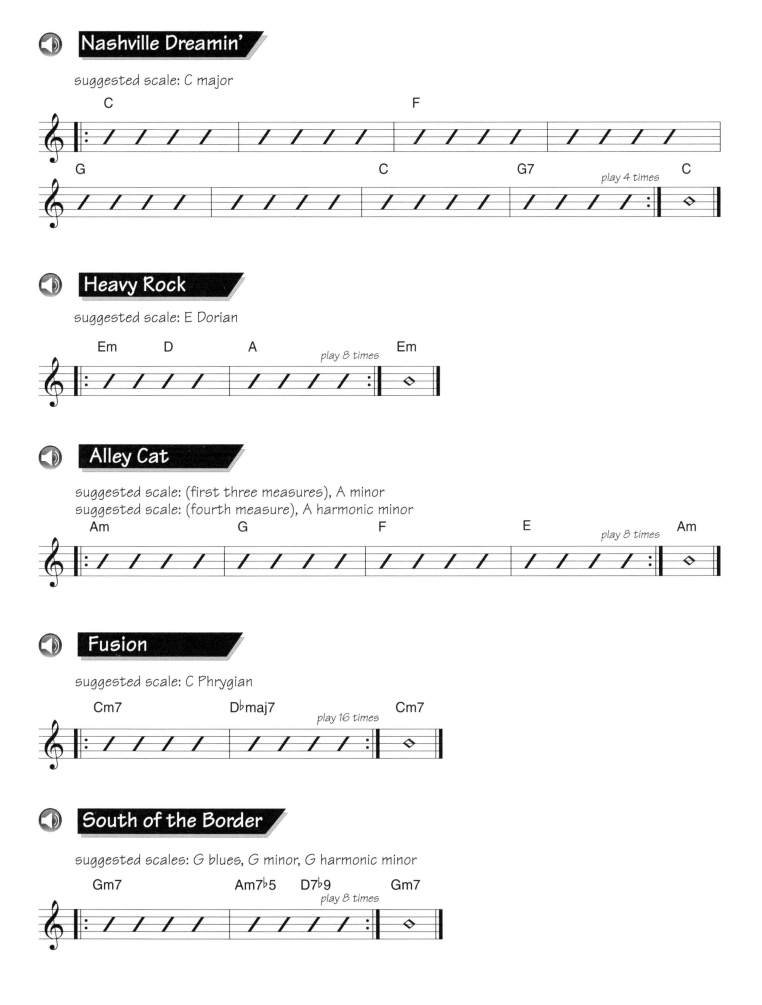

Heavy Rock

suggested scale: E Dorian

Alley Cat

suggested scale: (first three measures), A minor
suggested scale: (fourth measure), A harmonic minor

Fusion

suggested scale: C Phrygian

South of the Border

suggested scales: G blues, G minor, G harmonic minor

Don't stop there! Turn the page...

Scare Us

suggested scale/mode: A blues, B♭ Lydian

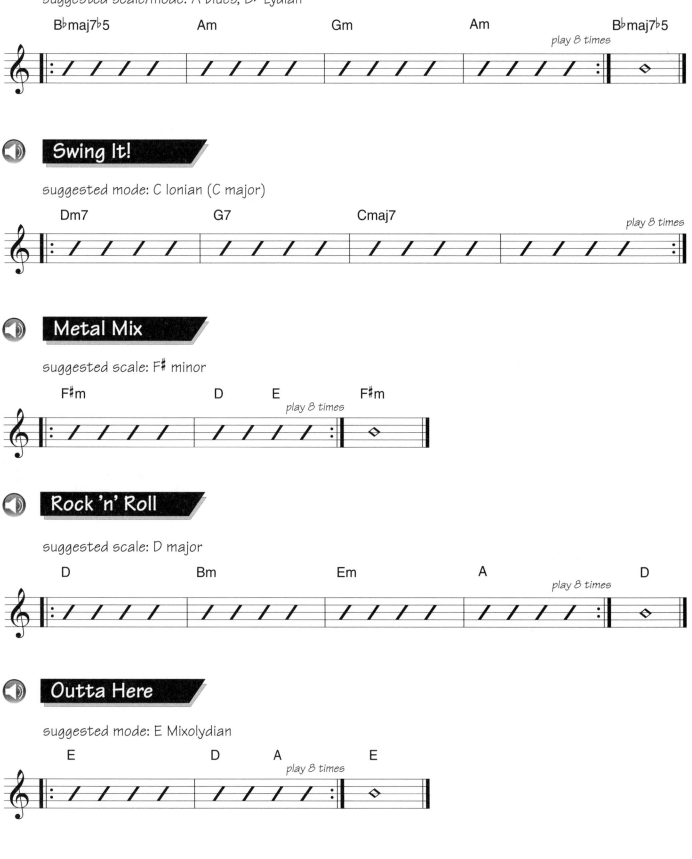

Bᵇmaj7♭5   Am   Gm   Am   *play 8 times*   Bᵇmaj7♭5

Swing It!

suggested mode: C Ionian (C major)

Dm7   G7   Cmaj7   *play 8 times*

Metal Mix

suggested scale: F♯ minor

F♯m   D   E   *play 8 times*   F♯m

Rock 'n' Roll

suggested scale: D major

D   Bm   Em   A   *play 8 times*   D

Outta Here

suggested mode: E Mixolydian

E   D   A   *play 8 times*   E

Bravo! You're ready for the big leagues…